NORO
LACE

NORO LACE

30 EXQUISITE KNITS

sixth&spring books
NEW YORK

Managing Editor	**LAURA COOKE**
Senior Editor	**LISA SILVERMAN**
Yarn Editor	**VANESSA PUTT**
Editorial Assistant	**JOHANNA LEVY**
Supervising Patterns Editor	**LORI STEINBERG**
Patterns Editors	**RENEE LORION**
	MARI LYNN PATRICK
	MARGEAU SOBOTI
Technical Illustrations	**LORETTA DACHMAN**
	RENEE LORION
Photography	**ROSE CALLAHAN**
Fashion Stylist	**JOANNA RADOW**
Assistant Stylist	**JENNA SLEVIN**
Hair and Makeup	**SOKPHALLA BAN**

**Assorted jewelry courtesy of
Rachel Reinhardt
rachelreinhardt.com**

Vice President	**TRISHA MALCOLM**
Publisher	**CAROLINE KILMER**
Creative Director	**JOE VIOR**
Production Manager	**DAVID JOINNIDES**
President	**ART JOINNIDES**
Chairman	**JAY STEIN**

Library of Congress Cataloging-in-Publication Data

Noro lace: 30 exquisite knits / the editors of Sixth&Spring Books.
pages cm
ISBN: 978-1-936096-85-5
1. Lace craft. 2. Knitting—Patterns. 3. Lace and lace making.
I. Sixth & Spring Books.
TT810.N67 2015
746.2'26—dc23

2014030169

Manufactured in China
1 3 5 7 9 10 8 6 4 2
First Edition

sixth&spring books

161 Avenue of the Americas • New York, New York 10013
sixthandspringbooks.com

CONTENTS

Introduction

Knitters have long been drawn to the elegance and the endless creative possibilities of lace. Now *Noro Lace* brings together top designers and one of the world's best-loved yarns to present a collection of knits that explore those possibilities—with breathtaking results. From simple mesh stitches that allow Noro's entrancing variegated colorways to shine, to complex, intricate patterns designed to work with the shifting hues in unexpected ways, these projects all use lace to bring out the beauty in Noro's luxurious fibers.

Eisaku Noro has been creating his world-renowned yarns in Japan's Aichi province for more than forty years. Spun from the finest natural materials with great respect for environmental concerns, these spectacular yarns are dyed exclusively by hand into a dazzling array of colors. As with *Knit Noro*, *Knit Noro 1 2 3 Skeins*, and the other titles in the collection, the projects in this book use several popular Noro yarns: various weights of the classics Silk Garden, Taiyo, and Kureyon, along with newer additions, such as the sublimely soft Shiraito and the rich, tonal Silk Garden Solo.

Many of today's most talented knitwear designers, including Deborah Newton, Laura Zukaite, Brooke Nico, and more, have been inspired to create stunning tops, eye-catching accessories, and statement home décor. Whether you're a lace lover who's just discovering the wonder of Noro yarn or you've been a Noro fan for years, *Noro Lace* will open your mind and take your knitting to new and beautiful places.

The Projects

Crescent Shawl

Crescent Shawl

A traditional Shetland lace pattern combines with stockinette sections in a shawl with a pretty shape and a pretty texture.

Designed by Lars Rains

Skill Level:

■■■□

Materials

- Two 1¾oz/50g hanks (each approx 196yd/180m) of Noro *Shiraito* (cashmere/angora/wool) in #37 **1**
- Size 8 (5mm) circular needle, 40"/100cm long, OR SIZE TO OBTAIN GAUGE
- Stitch markers

Size

Instructions are written for one size.

Knitted Measurements

Width along upper edge approx 60"/152.5cm
Length at center 9½"/24cm

Gauges

14 sts and 20 rows to 4"/10cm after blocking over chart pat using size 8 (5.5mm) needle.
14 sts and 25 rows to 4"/10cm after blocking over St st using size 8 (5.5mm) needle.
TAKE TIME TO CHECK GAUGES.

Notes

1) Shawl is worked back and forth in rows. Circular needle is used to accommodate large number of sts.
2) Shawl is worked from the back neck to the lower edge.

Shawl

Cast on 75 sts.
Next row (RS) Knit.
Next row K2, p1, place marker (pm), p2, *k2tog, yo, p1, yo, k2tog, p1; rep from * 10 times more, p1, pm, p1, k2.

Begin chart

Row 1 (RS) K2, (yo twice), k to marker, M1L, sl marker, work to rep line, work 6-st rep 10 times across, work to end of chart, sl marker, M1R, k to last 2 sts, (yo twice), k2.
Row 2 K3, p to marker, sl marker, work to rep line, work 6-st rep 10 times across, work to end of chart, sl marker, p to last 3 sts, k3.
Cont to work chart in this manner until row 4 is complete. Rep rows 1–4, working inc'd sts in St st (k on RS, p on WS), until piece measures 9"/23cm from beg, end with a chart row 4.
Knit 4 rows.
Bind off as foll: K2, *return sts to LH needle, k2tog tbl, k1; rep from * until st rem. Fasten off. ❖

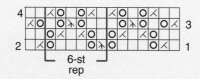

Stitch Key

☐ k on RS, p on WS

⊟ p on RS, k on WS

☑ yo

◿ k2tog on RS, k2tog on WS

◪ SK2P

Slouchy Cross Stitch Cap

Slouchy Cross Stitch Cap

A cross stitch pattern formed by elongated stitches adds lightness and graphic interest to a cozy slouchy hat.

Designed by Sarah Thieneman

Skill Level:
■■■□

Materials

- One 3½oz/100g skein (each approx 352yd/323m) of Noro *Taiyo Sport* (cotton/wool/silk/nylon) in #9 ②
- Sizes 4 and 5 (3.5 and 3.75mm) circular needles, 24"/60cm long, OR SIZE TO OBTAIN GAUGE
- One set (5) size 5 (3.75mm) double-pointed needles (dpns)
- Cable needle (cn)
- Stitch marker

Size
Instructions are written for one size, to fit adult woman.

Knitted Measurements
Brim circumference 22"/56cm
Length 10"/25.5cm

Gauge
20 sts and 24 rows to 4"/10cm over pat st using larger needles.
TAKE TIME TO CHECK GAUGE.

Pattern Stitch
(multiple of 6 sts plus 2)
Rnds 1–4 Knit.
Rnd 5 K1, *purl, wrapping yarn 3 times for each st; rep from * to last st, k1.
Rnd 6 K1, *sl 3 sts to cn, dropping extra wraps, and hold to *back*, p3, dropping extra wraps, p3 from cn; rep from * to last st, k1.
Rep rnds 1–6 for pat st.

Cap
With smaller needles, cast on 112 sts. Join, being careful not to twist sts, and place marker for beg of rnd.
Next rnd *K2, p2; rep from * around.
Rep this rnd 11 times more for k2, p2 rib.
Next (dec) rnd Work in rib to last 4 sts, k2tog, p2tog—110 sts.

Begin pat st
Work rnds 1–6 of pat st 6 times.

Shape crown
Note Change to dpns when sts no longer fit comfortably on circular needle.
Next (dec) rnd K1, [k2tog] 54 times, k1—56 sts.
Rep rnds 1–6 of pat st.
Next (dec) rnd K4, [k2tog] 24 times, k4—32 sts.
Rep rnds 1–6 of pat st.
Next (dec) rnd [K2tog] 16 times—16 sts.
Break yarn, leaving a long tail. Thread tail through rem sts to close. ✤

Cropped Cardi

Cropped Cardi

The classic cropped cardi gets a fresh look with stripes of lace and stockinette, a bobble lace border, and a snap closure.

Designed by Anna Davis

Skill Level:
■■■□

Materials
- 5 (6, 6, 7, 7, 8) 1¾oz/50g skeins (each approx 108yd/99m) of Noro *Silk Garden* (silk/mohair/wool) in #84 ④
- Size 7 (4.5mm) circular needle, 32"/80cm long, OR SIZE TO OBTAIN GAUGE
- One ½"/1.25cm snap
- Stitch markers, stitch holders

Sizes
Instructions are written for X-Small (Small, Medium, Large, X-Large, XX-Large). Shown in size X-Small.

Knitted Measurements
Width 34½ (37, 39¾, 42¼, 45, 47½)"/87.5 (94, 101, 108, 114, 120.5)cm
Length 15½ (15½, 16, 16¼, 17, 17½)"/39.5 (39.5, 40.5, 42, 43, 44.5)cm
Upper arm 14 (14, 15, 16, 17, 18)"/35.5 (35.5, 38, 40.5, 43, 45.5)cm

Gauge
17 sts and 24 rows to 4"/10cm over St st using size 7 (4.5mm) needles. TAKE TIME TO CHECK GAUGE.

Sloped Bind-Off
One row before the next bind-off row, work to the last st of row. Do not work this st. Turn work. With yarn in back, sl first st purlwise from LH needle. Pass the unworked st of previous row over the slipped st. The first st is bound off. Bind off the remaining number of sts in that row in the normal way.

Stitch Glossary
MB (make bobble) [K1, p1] 3 times in next st, turn, k6, turn, pass 5 sts over first st one at a time, p1 tbl.

Scalloped Floral Lace Border
(multiple of 11 sts plus 4)
Row 1 (RS) Knit.
Row 2 (WS) Knit.
Row 3 K1, *k5, k2tog, yo, k4; rep from * to last 3 sts, k3.
Row 4 and all WS rows Purl.
Row 5 K1, *k4, k2tog, yo, k1, yo, ssk, k2; rep from * to last 3 sts, k3.
Row 7 K1, *k3, [k2tog, yo] twice, k1, yo, ssk, k1; rep from * to last 3 sts, k3.
Row 9 K1, *k2, [k2tog, yo] twice, k1, [yo, ssk] twice; rep from * to last 3 sts, k3.
Row 11 K1, *k3, k2tog, yo, k1, MB, k1, yo, ssk, k1; rep from * to last 3 sts, k3.
Row 13 K1, *k4, MB, k3, MB, k2; rep from * to last 3 sts, k3.
Row 15 K1, *k6, MB, k4; rep from * to last 3 sts, k3.
Row 16 Purl.

Vertical Lace Trellis
(over an odd number of sts)
Rows 1 and 3 (WS) Purl.
Row 2 K2, *yo, k2tog; rep from * to last st, k1.
Row 4 K1, *ssk, yo; rep from * to last 2 sts, k2.
Rep rows 1–4 for vertical lace trellis.

Notes
1) Cardigan is worked back and forth in one piece to the underarm, then divided to work fronts and back separately to shoulder.
2) Use sloped bind-off method for all shaping.

Body
Cast on 147 (158, 169, 180, 191, 202) sts. Work 16 rows of scalloped floral lace border. Work 3 rows in St st (k on RS, p on WS), end with a RS row.

Begin alternating stripe pat
*Work 8 rows in vertical lace trellis, 6 rows in St st; rep from * for

alternating stripe pat until piece measures 8½"/21.5cm from beg, end with a RS row.

Next row (WS) Work 37 (39, 42, 45, 48, 50) sts for left front, place marker (pm), work 73 (80, 85, 90, 95, 102) sts for back, pm, work 37 (39, 42, 45, 48, 50) sts for right front.

Divide for fronts and back

Next row (RS) [Work to 2 (2, 3, 4, 5, 5) sts before marker, bind off 2 (2, 3, 4, 5, 5) sts, remove marker, bind off 2 (2, 3, 4, 5, 5) sts] twice, work to end.

Next row (WS) Work 35 (37, 39, 41, 43, 45) left front sts, turn, leaving back and right front sts on hold.

Left front

Bind off 2 (2, 3, 4, 5, 5) sts at beg of next row—33 (35, 36, 37, 38, 40) sts. Cont in alternating stripe pat, dec'ing 0 (0, 1, 0, 1, 1) st on last St st row of foll stripe—33 (35, 35, 37, 37, 39) sts. Work even until armhole measures 3 (3, 3½, 4, 4½, 5)"/7.5 (7.5, 9, 10, 11.5, 12.5)cm, end with a RS row.

Neck shaping

Bind off 4 (3, 3, 5, 4, 4) sts at neck edge once, then 2 sts 7 times—15 (18, 18, 18, 19, 21) sts.
Work even until armhole measures 7 (7, 7½, 8, 8½, 9)"/18 (18, 19, 20.5, 21.5, 23)cm, end with a WS row.
Bind off 8 (9, 9, 9, 9, 10) sts at beg of next row. Bind off rem 7 (9, 9, 9, 10, 11) sts.

Back

Rejoin yarn to 69 (76, 79, 82, 85, 92) sts on hold for back, ready to work a WS row. Bind off 2 (2, 3, 4, 5, 5) sts at beg of next 2 rows—65 (72, 73, 74, 75, 82) sts.
Cont in alternating stripe pat, dec'ing 0 (1, 0, 1, 0, 1) st on last St st row of foll stripe—65 (71, 73, 73, 75, 81) sts.
Work even until armhole measures 7 (7, 7½, 8, 8½, 9)"/18 (18, 19, 20.5, 21.5, 23)cm, end with a WS row.
Next row (RS) Work 15 (18, 18, 18, 19, 21) sts, bind off center 35 (35, 37, 37, 37, 39) sts, work to end. Work shoulder sts separately as foll:
Next row (WS) Bind off 8 (9, 9, 9, 9, 10) sts, work to end of first side. Turn and bind off rem 7 (9, 9, 9, 10, 11) sts.
Rejoin yarn to left shoulder sts, ready to work a WS row. Work 1 WS row. Bind off 8 (9, 9, 9, 9, 10) sts at beg of next row. Bind off rem 7 (9, 9, 9, 10, 11) sts.

Right front

Rejoin yarn to 35 (37, 39, 41, 43, 45) sts on hold for right front ready to work a WS row. Bind off 2 (2, 3, 4, 5, 5) sts at beg of next row, work to end—33 (35, 36, 37, 38, 40) sts. Cont in alternating stripe pat,

dec'ing 0 (0, 1, 0, 1, 1) st on last St st row of foll stripe—33 (35, 35, 37, 37, 39) sts. Work even until armhole measures 3 (3, 3½, 4, 4½, 5)"/7.5 (7.5, 9, 10, 11.5, 12.5)cm, end with a WS row.
Complete as for left front, reversing all shaping.

Sleeves

Cast on 70 (70, 70, 70, 81, 81) sts. Work 16 rows of scalloped floral lace border. Work 3 rows in St st, end with a RS row and dec 1 (dec 1, inc 5, inc 1, 0, 0) st on last row—69 (69, 75, 71, 81, 81) sts.

Begin alternating stripe pat

*Work 8 rows in vertical lace trellis, 6 rows in St st; rep from * for alternating stripe pat, AT THE SAME TIME, inc 1 st each side every 0 (0, 0, other, other, other) row 0 (0, 0, 6, 6, 8) times—69 (69, 75, 83, 93, 97) sts. Work even until piece measures 6 (6, 6½, 7, 7, 7)"/15 (15, 16.5, 18, 18, 18)cm from beg, end with a WS row.
Bind off 2 (2, 3, 4, 5, 5) sts at beg of next 4 rows—61 (61, 63, 67, 73, 77) sts. Bind off.

Finishing

Block pieces lightly to measurements. Sew shoulder seams. Sew sleeves into armholes. Sew sleeve seams.

Front bands

With RS facing, beg at lower edge, pick up and k 46 (46, 48, 50, 52, 54) sts along right front neck edge. Knit 3 rows. Bind off loosely. Beg at neck edge, rep for left front.

Neckband

With RS facing, beg at upper edge of right front band, pick up and k 32 sts along shaped right neck edge to shoulder, 36 (36, 38, 38, 38, 40) sts along back neck edge, 32 sts along shaped left neck edge to left front band—100 (100, 102, 102, 102, 104) sts. Knit 3 rows. Bind off loosely.
Sew halves of snap in place at neck edge. ❖

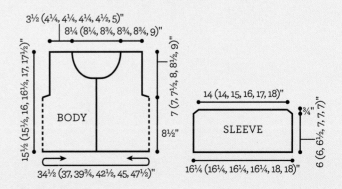

Mock Neck Capelet

Mock Neck Capelet

Ribs flow from the shoulders up to a mock turtleneck collar atop a wavy lace capelet.

Designed by Sandi Prosser

Skill Level:
■■■□

Materials

- 2 (3, 3) 3½oz/100g skeins (each approx 328yd/300m) of Noro *Silk Garden Sock* (wool/silk/nylon/mohair) in #269 **1**
- Size 5 (3.75mm) circular needle, 24"/60cm long, OR SIZE TO OBTAIN GAUGE
- Size 3 (3.25mm) circular needle, 16"/40cm long (for size Small only)
- Size 5 (3.75mm) circular needle, 16"/40cm long (for sizes Medium and Large only)
- Stitch markers

Sizes

Instructions are written for Small (Medium, Large). Shown in size Small.

Knitted Measurements

Circumference at lower edge after blocking 42 (48, 54)"/106.5 (122, 137)cm
Length 18 (18½, 19)"/45.5 (47, 48)cm

Gauge

24 sts and 34 rnds to 4"/10cm over chart 1 after blocking using size 5 (3.75mm) needle. TAKE TIME TO CHECK GAUGE.

Capelet

With longer circular needle, cast on 255 (289, 323) sts.

Begin chart 1

Rnd 1 Work 17-st rep 15 (17, 19) times around.
Cont to work chart in this manner until rnd 36 is complete, then rep rnds 6–36 once more.

Begin chart 2

Rnd 1 Work st-rep 15 (17, 19) times around.
Cont to work chart in this manner until rnd 11 is complete—195 (221, 247) sts.

Collar

Next (dec) rnd Knit, dec 3 (4, 7) sts evenly around—192 (217, 240) sts.
Next rnd *P3, k3 (4, 5); rep from * around.
Next rnd Knit.
Rep last 2 rnds 10 times more.
Next (dec) rnd *P3, k2tog, k1 (2, 3); rep from * around—160 (186, 210) sts.
Next rnd Knit.
Next rnd *P3, k2 (3, 4); rep from * around.
Rep last 2 rnds 8 times more.

For sizes Medium and Large only
Knit 1 rnd.
Next (dec) rnd *P3, k2tog, k1 (2); rep from * around—155 (180) sts.
Next rnd Knit.
Next rnd *P3, k2 (3); rep from * around.
Rep last 2 rnds once more.

For size Large only
Knit 1 rnd.
Next (dec) rnd *P3, k2tog, k1; rep from * around—150 sts.

Next rnd Knit.
Next rnd *P3, k2; rep from * around.
Rep last 2 rnds once more.

For all sizes
Change to shorter circular needle.
Next (dec) rnd *P1, p2tog, k2; rep from * around—128 (124, 120) sts.
Next rnd *P2, k2; rep from * around.
Next rnd Knit.
Rep last 2 rnds until piece measures 18 (18½, 19)"/45.5 (47, 48)cm
from beg. Bind off. ❖

CHART 1

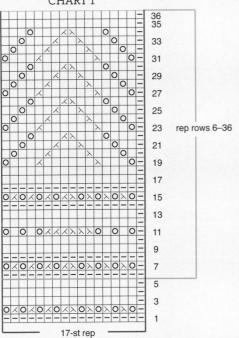

rep rows 6–36

17-st rep

CHART 2

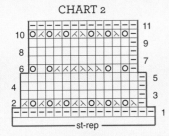

st-rep

Stitch Key

☐	knit
⊟	purl
⊠	k2tog
⊠	ssk
⊙	yo

Bobble Band Scarf

Bobble Band Scarf

A tweedy tonal yarn shows off the textures of a scarf with bands of lace and bobbles alternating with reverse stockinette.

Designed by Laura Zukaite

Skill Level:
■■■□

Materials
- Six 1¾oz/50g skeins (each approx 109yd/100m) of Noro *Silk Garden Solo* (silk/mohair/wool) in #4 **4**
- One pair size 7 (4.5mm) needles OR SIZE TO OBTAIN GAUGE
- Stitch markers
- Scrap yarn

Size
Instructions are written for one size.

Knitted Measurements
Width 13"/33cm
Length 71"/180.5cm

Gauges
20 sts and 20 rows to 4"/10cm over bobble lace pat using size 7 (4.5mm) needles.
17 sts and 22 rows to 4"/10cm over St st using size 7 (4.5mm) needles.
TAKE TIME TO CHECK GAUGES.

Stitch Glossary
MB (make bobble) (K1, yo, k1, yo, k1) in same stitch, turn and p5, turn and k5, turn and p5, turn and ssk, k1, k2tog, turn and p3tog, turn and, with yarn in back, sl bobble stitch onto RH needle.

Bobble Lace Pattern
(multiple of 10 sts plus 1)
Row 1 (RS) P1, *yo, ssk, p5, k2tog, yo, p1; rep from * to end.
Row 2 K1, *k1, p1, k5, p1, k2; rep from * to end.
Row 3 P1, *p1, yo, ssk, p3, k2tog, yo, p2; rep from * to end.
Row 4 K1, *k2, p1, k3, p1, k3; rep from * to end.
Row 5 P1, *p2, yo, ssk, p1, k2tog, yo, p3; rep from * to end.
Row 6 K1, *k3, p1, k1, p1, k4; rep from * to end.
Row 7 P1, *p3, yo, S2KP, yo, p3, MB; rep from *, end last rep p4.
Row 8 K1, *k3, p3, k3, p1tbl (in bobble st); rep from *, end last rep k4.
Row 9 P1, *p2, k2tog, yo, p1, yo, ssk, p3; rep from * to end.
Row 10 K1, *k2, p1, k3, p1, k3; rep from * to end.
Row 11 P1, *p1, k2tog, yo, p3, yo, ssk, p2; rep from * to end.
Row 12 K1, *k1, p1, k5, p1, k2; rep from * to end.
Row 13 P1, *k2tog, yo, p5, yo, ssk, p1; rep from * to end.
Row 14 K1, *p1, k7, p1, k1; rep from * to end.
Row 15 K2tog, *yo, p3, MB, p3, yo, S2KP; rep from *, end yo, p3, MB, p3, yo, ssk.
Row 16 P1, *p1, k3, p1tbl (in bobble st), k3, p2; rep from * to end.
Rep rows 1–16 for bobble lace pat.

Scarf
Cast on 57 sts. Knit 4 rows (for garter st).
Row 1 (RS) Sl 1, p1, k1, p to last 3 sts, k1, p1, k1.
Row 2 Sl 1, k1, p1, k to last 3 sts, p1, k1, p1.
Rep these 2 rows for rev St st pat for 2½"/6.5cm, end with a WS row.

Begin bobble lace pat
*Next row (RS) Sl 1, p1, k1, work first st of bobble lace pat, work
10-st rep 5 times across, k1, p1, k1.
Cont to work bobble lace pat in this manner, working first and last 3 sts of every row in rib as established, until row 16 is complete. Then rep rows 1–6 once more.
Next row (RS) Sl 1, p1, k1, p1, [p3, yo, SK2P, yo, p4] 5 times, k1, p1, k1.**
Work in rev St st pat for 5"/12.5cm.*
Rep from * to * 5 times more, then work from * to ** once. Work in rev St st pat for 2½"/6.5cm. Knit 4 rows. Bind off loosely knitwise. ❧

Tabard with Cowl

Tabard with Cowl

Zigzag borders on the body and separate cowl echo the diamond lace pattern on a striking tabard top.

Designed by Deborah Newton

Skill Level:
■■■□

Materials
- 6 (6, 7, 8) 3½oz/100g balls (each approx 220yd/200m) of Noro *Taiyo* (cotton/silk/wool/polyamide) in #25 ④
- One size 7 (4.5mm) needles OR SIZE TO OBTAIN GAUGE
- One size 7 (4.5mm) circular needle, 24"/60cm long
- Nine 1"/25mm toggle buttons
- Stitch markers

Sizes
Instructions are written for X-Small/Small (Medium, Large/X-Large, 1X/2X). Shown in size Medium.

Knitted Measurements
Bust (buttoned) 38 (40, 45, 51)"/96.5 (101.5, 114, 129.5)cm
Length 25"/63.5cm

Gauge
25 sts to 6"/15cm and 24 rows to 4"/10cm over lace chart using size 7 (4.5mm) needles. TAKE TIME TO CHECK GAUGE.

Notes
1) Measurements do not include k1 selvage st at each side of pieces.
2) Zigzag border is picked up and knit when front and back pieces are complete.

Back
Cast on 76 (81, 92, 103) sts.
Set-up row (WS) P10 (7, 7, 7), place marker (pm), p56 (67, 78, 89), pm, p10 (7, 7, 7).

Begin chart
Row 1 (RS) K10 (7, 7, 7), sl marker, work 11-st rep 5 (6, 7, 8) times across, work to end of chart, sl marker, k10 (7, 7, 7).
Cont to work in this manner, with sts as established in St st or chart pat, until row 16 is complete. Rep rows 1–16 until piece measures 13½ (13, 12½, 12)"/34 (33, 32, 30.5)cm from beg, end with a WS row.

Armhole shaping
Bind off 2 sts at beg of next 2 rows—72 (77, 88, 99) sts.
Dec row (RS) K1, ssk, work to last 3 sts, k2tog, k1—2 sts dec'd.
Rep dec row every other row 4 (3, 3, 3) times more—62 (69, 80, 91) sts.
Work even until armhole measures 8 (8¼, 9, 9½)"/20.5 (21.5, 24, 25.5)cm, end with a row 16. Piece measures approx 21½"/54.5cm from beg. Pm to mark the center 30 (31, 32, 31) sts on the last WS row.

Neck shaping
Note For all sizes, only the first and last 1 (1, 1, 2) sets of sts will cont in the chart pat and the center sts will be worked in St st while shaping the neck.
Next row (RS) Work to center marked sts, join a 2nd ball of yarn, and bind off center 30 (31, 32, 31) sts, work to end. Working both sides at once, bind off 2 sts from each neck edge 3 times—10 (13, 18, 24) sts rem each side. Armhole measures 9 (9½, 10, 10½)"/23 (24, 25.5, 26.5)cm.

Shoulder shaping
Bind off 3 (4, 6, 8) sts from each shoulder edge twice, then 4 (5, 6, 8) sts once.

Front
Work same as back.

Zigzag border
Note Border is worked over 1 group of 14 sts at a time.

From the RS, pick up and k 84 (84, 98, 112) sts along lower edge of front.
Row 1 (WS) K14, turn.
**Row 2 (dec RS) K1, ssk, k to last 3 sts, k2tog, k1—2 sts dec'd.
Row 3 Knit.
Rep rows 2 and 3 until 4 sts rem, end with a WS row.
Next row (RS) K1, k2tog, k1—3 sts.
Next row (WS) Bind off 2 sts, with 1 st rem on needle; then with WS facing, beg along the left edge of the base of the just-worked zigzag point, sl the tip of LH needle into 1 garter bump on edge of each of the 6 garter ridges (for a total of 7 sts); then bind off 6 sts so that 1 st rem on the RH needle; then, working into the next st on the needle, bind off this st on needle to connect to the next zigzag, then k 13 more sts—14 sts on RH needle, turn, then beg at **, work the next zigzag in same way. Rep from ** until 6 (6, 7, 8) zigzag pats are completed *and* on the last zigzag pat, after binding off 6 sts, break yarn and pull through last st to fasten off. Work back edge same as front.

Finishing
Sew one shoulder seam.

Neckband
With circular needle and RS facing, pick up and k 111 (114, 116, 114) sts evenly around neck edge. Knit 5 rows. Bind off. Sew other shoulder and neckband seam.

Armhole trims
With circular needle and RS facing, pick up and k 84 (90, 95, 101) sts evenly around armhole. Knit 5 rows. Bind off.

Back button bands
From the RS, beg above the zigzag border, pick up and k 64 (62, 59, 57) sts along one back edge up to the end of the armhole trim. Knit 7 rows. Bind off.

Left front buttonhole band
From the RS, pick up and k 64 (62, 59, 57) sts along the left front edge up to the end of the armhole trim.
Buttonhole row (WS) K4, bind off 4 sts for buttonhole, [k13 (12, 11, 11), bind off 4 sts for buttonhole] 3 times, k to end. On next row, cast on 4 sts over each set of buttonholes. Knit 5 rows more. Bind off.

Right front buttonhole band
Pick up as for left front buttonhole band.
Buttonhole row (WS) K5 (6, 6, 4), [bind off 4 sts for buttonhole, k13 (12, 11, 11)] 3 times, bind off 4 sts for buttonhole, k to end. Finish as for left front buttonhole band. Sew on buttons.

Cowl
Cast on 34 sts. Purl 1 row.

Begin chart
Row 1 (RS) Work the 11-st rep 3 times across, work to end of chart. Work even in lace pat, foll chart, until piece measures approx 29"/73.5cm from beg, end with a row 16. Bind off.

Zigzag trim—long edges
From the RS, pick up and k 126 sts along one long edge of cowl. Foll border instructions for tabard, work zigzag trim with 9 zigzags of 14 sts each. Work other long edge in same way.

Zigzag trim—short ends
From the RS, pick up and k 42 sts along one short end of cowl. Work 3 zigzags as for previous trims, pick up and work the other short end in same manner until there are 3 rows worked in the first zigzag and 10 sts rem. Pm to mark the 4 center sts.
Buttonhole row (RS) Work zigzag pat row as established to the center 4 sts, bind off 4 sts, work to end.
On next row, cast on 4 sts over the bound-off sts. Complete the 3 zigzags as before. ❖

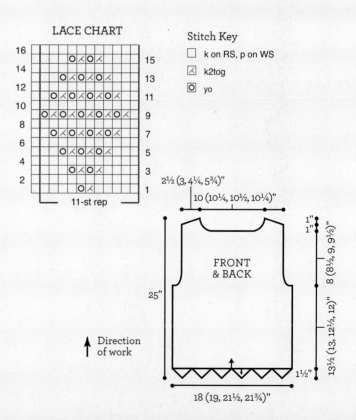

LACE CHART

Stitch Key
☐ k on RS, p on WS
◩ k2tog
◉ yo

11-st rep

2½ (3, 4¼, 5¾)"

10 (10¼, 10½, 10¼)"

1"
1"

FRONT & BACK

25"

↑ Direction of work

8 (8½, 9, 9½)"

13½ (13, 12½, 12)"

1½"

18 (19, 21½, 21¾)"

Textured Mittens

Textured Mittens

Elegant mittens acheive balance with both airy lace and plush bobbles on the hands and cuffs.

Designed by Pat Olski

Skill Level:
■■■■

Materials
- One 3½oz/100g skein (each approx 350yd/320m) of Noro *Taiyo Sport* (cotton/silk/wool/polyamide) in #10 2
- One set (5) each sizes 2 and 3 (2.75 and 3.25mm) double-pointed needles (dpns) OR SIZE TO OBTAIN GAUGE
- Stitch markers
- Scrap yarn

Size
Instructions are written for one size, to fit adult woman.

Knitted Measurements
Hand circumference above thumb 7½"/19cm
Length 11½"/29cm

Gauge
20 sts and 31 rnds to 4"/10cm over St st using larger needles. TAKE TIME TO CHECK GAUGE.

Stitch Glossary
MB (make bobble) (K1, p1, k1, p1, k1) in same st. In next rnd, k5tog to complete bobble.

Note
Chart can be found on page 134.

Right Mitten
Cuff
With larger needles, cast on 40 sts. Join, being careful not to twist sts, and place marker (pm) for beg of rnd.
Next rnd *P1, k1; rep from * around.
Rep last rnd for p1, k1 rib for 2 rnds more.
Next (eyelet) rnd *[P1, k1] twice, k2tog, yo; rep from * twice more, rib to end.
Next rnd *P1, k1; rep from * around.
Rep last 2 rows 7 times more.
Next (dec) rnd Knit, dec 6 sts evenly around—34 sts.
Change to smaller needles.
Next rnd Purl.
Knit 5 rnds.
Next rnd Purl.
Knit 2 rnds.
Change to larger needles.

Begin chart
Rnd 1 (inc) Work chart pat over 17 sts, k2, pm (1st gusset marker), M1, k1, M1, pm (2nd gusset marker), k to end of rnd—36 sts.
Work 3 rnds even, working chart rows over first 17 sts in each rnd.
Next (inc) rnd Work in pat to 1st gusset marker, sl marker, M1, k to 2nd gusset marker, M1, sl marker, k to end of rnd—2 sts inc'd.
Cont to work chart in this way, rep inc rnd every 4th rnd 3 times more—11 sts between gusset markers.
Next rnd Work in pat to 2nd gusset marker, place 11 gusset sts just worked on scrap yarn for thumb, work to end of rnd.

Next rnd Work chart rnd over 17 sts, k to thumb opening, pm, cast on 5 sts, work to end of rnd—38 sts.

Work 1 rnd even.

Next (dec) rnd Work chart rnd over 17 sts, k to marker, sl marker, ssk, k1, k2tog, k to end of rnd—36 sts.

Work 1 rnd even.

Next (dec) rnd Work chart rnd over 17 sts, k to marker, remove marker, SK2P, k to end of rnd—34 sts.

Work even in pat until rnd 45 of chart is complete.

Work even if necessary in St st (k every rnd) until piece measures 10"/25.5cm from beg.

Next rnd K17, pm, k to end of rnd.

Shape top

Next (dec) rnd [Ssk, k to 2 sts before next marker, k2tog] twice— 4 sts dec'd.

Rep dec rnd every other rnd twice more, then every rnd 3 times— 10 sts.

Break yarn, leaving a long tail. Thread tail through open sts to close top.

Thumb

Place thumb sts on larger dpn, pick up and k 4 sts along thumb opening—15 sts.

Divide sts evenly on 3 dpns. Work in St st until thumb measures 2"/5cm.

Next rnd [K2tog, k3] 3 times around—12 sts.

Next rnd [K2tog, k2] 3 times around—9 sts.

Next rnd [K2tog, k1] 3 times around—6 sts.

Break yarn, leaving a long tail. Thread tail through open sts to close thumb.

Left Mitten

Work as for right mitten to begin chart.

Begin chart

Rnd 1 (inc) Work chart pat over 17 sts, k16, pm (1st gusset marker), M1, k1, M1, pm (2nd gusset marker), k to end of rnd.

Complete as for right mitten. ❖

Eyelet Wave Cowl

Eyelet Wave Cowl

A simple lace repeat with a bias tilt creates undulating columns in a roomy, easy-to-knit cowl.

Designed by Bonnie Franz

Skill Level:
■■□□

Materials
■ Two 3½oz/100g skeins (each approx 327yd/300m) of Noro *Taiyo* (cotton/silk/wool/polyamide) in #23 ④
■ Size 9 (5.5mm) circular needle, 24"/60cm long, OR SIZE TO OBTAIN GAUGE
■ Stitch marker

Size
Instructions are written for one size.

Knitted Measurements
Circumference 40"/101.5cm
Length 12"/30.5cm

Gauge
11 sts and 20 rnds to 4"/10cm after blocking over lace pat using size 9 (5.5mm) needles.
TAKE TIME TO CHECK GAUGE.

Lace Pattern
(multiple of 10 sts)
Rnd 1 *P1, yo, k3, ssk, 4; rep from * around.
Rnd 2 and all even-numbered rnds *P1, k9; rep from * around.
Rnd 3 *P1, k1, yo, k3, ssk, k3; rep from * around.
Rnd 5 *P1, k2, yo, k3, ssk, k2; rep from * around.
Rnd 7 *P1, k3, yo, k3, ssk, k1; rep from * around.
Rnd 9 *P1, k4, yo, k3, ssk; rep from * around.
Rnds 11 and 12 Knit.
Rep rows 1–12 for lace pat.

Note
Lace pat may be worked from chart *or* text.

Cowl
Cast on 110 sts. Join, being careful not to twist sts, and place marker for beg of rnd.
P 1 rnd, k 1 rnd, p 1 rnd.

Begin lace pat
Rnd 1 Work 10-st rep 11 times around.
Cont to work pat in this manner until rnd 12 is complete.
Rep rnds 1–12 four times more.
P 1 rnd, k 1 rnd, p 1 rnd.
Bind off.

Finishing
Block gently, allowing lower edge to scallop. ❧

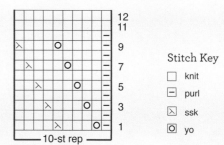

Stitch Key

□ knit
– purl
ᐳ ssk
Ⓞ yo

10-st rep

Wavy Stolette

Wavy Stolette

Undulating stockinette bands provide structure between lace panels in a sweet stole.

Designed by Robyn Schrager

Skill Level:
■■■□

Materials
- Two 3½oz/100g skeins (each approx 327d/300m) of Noro *Silk Garden Sock* (wool/silk/polyamide/mohair) in #S268 ⑪
- One pair size 5 (3.75mm) needles OR SIZE TO OBTAIN GAUGE
- Size F/5 (3.75mm) crochet hook
- Scrap yarn
- Removable stitch markers

Size
Instructions are written for one size.

Knitted Measurements
Width at deepest point 9"/23cm
Length 66"/167.5cm

Gauge
20 sts and 30 rows to 4"/10cm over chart pat using size 5 (3.75mm) needles. TAKE TIME TO CHECK GAUGE.

Provisional Cast-On
Using scrap yarn and crochet hook, chain the number of sts to cast on, plus a few extra. Cut a tail and pull the tail through the last chain. With knitting needle and yarn, pick up and knit the stated number of sts through the "purl bumps" on the back of the chain. To remove scrap chain, when instructed, pull out the tail from the last crochet st. Gently and slowly pull on the tail to unravel the crochet sts, carefully placing each released knit st on a needle.

Notes
1) Piece is worked with an I-cord edge along the lower edge and a slip st selvage st along the upper edge.
2) Chart can be found on page 134.

Stolette
Cast on 45 sts using provisional cast-on method. Purl 1 row.

Begin chart
Row 1 (RS) K3, work to rep line, work 16-st rep twice, work to end of chart, sl 1 wyif.
Row 2 K1, work to rep line, work 16-st rep twice, work to end of chart, sl 3 wyif.
Cont to work chart in this manner until row 16 is complete. Rep rows 1–16 until piece measures approx 18"/45.5cm from beg, end with a WS row. Place marker in end of this row.

Shape front
Next (dec) row (RS) Cont in pat to last 3 sts, k2tog, sl 1 wyif—1 st dec'd. Rep dec row every other row 15 times more—29 sts.
Cont in pat as established until piece measures 24"/61cm from marker, end with a WS row. Bind off loosely.

Second side
Carefully remove scrap yarn from provisional cast-on and place 45 sts on needle ready to work a RS row.
Row 1 (RS) K1, work to rep line, work 16-st chart rep twice, work to end of chart, sl 3 wyib.
Row 2 P3, work to rep line, work 16-st chart rep twice, work to end of chart, sl 1 wyif.
Cont to work chart in this manner until row 6 is complete.

Shape front
Next (dec) row (RS) K1, ssk, work to end—1 st dec'd.
Rep dec row every other row 15 times more—29 sts.
Cont in pat as established until 2nd side measures same as first side. Bind off loosely. ❦

Drape Front Blouse

Drape Front Blouse

A stunning and wearable top combines overlapping lapels with lacy dolman sleeves and a slightly cropped silhouette.

Designed by Brooke Nico

Skill Level:

■■■■

Materials

- 8 (10) 1¾oz/50g hanks (each approx 197yd/180m) of Noro *Shiraito* (cashmere/angora/wool) in #31 ■
- Size 5 (3.75mm) circular needles, 24 and 60"/60 and 150cm long, OR SIZE TO OBTAIN GAUGE
- Stitch markers and stitch holders

Sizes

Instructions are written for Small/Medium (Large/X-Large). Shown in size Small/Medium.

Knitted Measurements

Waist 30 (38)"/76 (96.5)cm
Length 17 (20¾)"/43 (52.5)cm

Gauge

20 sts and 30 rows to 4"/10cm over chart pats after blocking using size 5 (3.75mm) needles. TAKE TIME TO CHECK GAUGE.

Stitch Glossary

Make nupp (K1, yo, k1, yo, k1) in next st—5 sts made in 1 st. On following row, purl these 5 sts tog.

Lace Pattern

(multiple of 5 sts)
Row 1 (RS) *K2tog, yo, k1, yo, ssk; rep from * to end.
Row 2 (WS) K the knit sts and p the purl sts and yarn overs.
Rep rows 1 and 2 for lace pat.

Notes

1) Top is worked in one piece to the underarm, then fronts and back are worked separately to shoulder.
2) Schematic can be found on page 135.

Top

With longer circular needle, cast on 31 sts for left lapel, place marker (pm), cast on 23 (45) sts for left front, pm, cast on 67 (111) sts for back, pm, cast on 23 (45) sts for right front, pm, cast on 31 sts for right lapel—175 (263) sts. Purl 1 WS row.

For size Small/Medium only
Beg charts
Row 1 (RS) *K2, yo; rep from * to 1 st before marker, k1, sl marker, work right front chart to rep line, work 22-st rep, work to end of chart, sl marker, work back chart 1 to rep line, work 22-st rep 3 times across, work to end of chart, sl marker, work left front chart 1 to rep line, work 22-s rep, work to end of chart, sl marker, k1, *yo, k2; rep from * to end.
Row 2 and all WS rows Work in chart pats as established, k the knit sts and p the purl sts and yos over lapel sts.
Row 3 *K2, yo, k1, yo; rep from * to 1 st before marker, k1, work charts as established to last marker, [k1, yo] twice, *k2, yo, k1, yo; rep from * to last 2 sts, k2—76 sts lapel sts each side.
Row 5 K1, work row 1 of lace pat to marker, work charts as established to last marker, work row 1 of lace pat to last st, k1.
Row 6 Rep row 2.
Cont to work pats in this way, working lace pat over lapel sts each side and chart pats over rem sts, through row 46 of chart 1. Then rep rows 7-45 of charts once more, working 1 additional 22-st rep for fronts and 2 additional reps for back—71 sts for each front, 163 sts for back, 76 sts for each lapel.

For size Large/X-Large only
Note After the first 6 rows, one 40-row rep of charts is worked even, without increasing at side edges. After row 6 of charts, work chart only over 22-st repeats and work sts outside reps in St st.

Beg charts
Row 1 (RS) *K2, yo; rep from * to 1 st before marker, k1, sl marker, work right front chart 1 to rep line, work 22-st rep twice across, work to end of chart, sl marker, work back chart 1 to rep line, work 22-st rep 5 times across, work to end of chart, sl marker, work left front chart 1 to rep line, work 22-st rep twice across, work to end of chart, sl marker, k1, *yo, k2; rep from * to end.
Row 2 and all WS rows Work in chart pats as established, k the knit sts and p the purl sts and yos over lapel sts.
Row 3 *K2, yo, k1, yo; rep from * to 1 st before marker, k1, work charts as established to last marker, [k1, yo] twice, *k2, yo, k1, yo; rep from * to last 2 sts, k2—76 lapel sts each side.
Row 5 K1, work row 1 of lace pat to marker, work charts as established to last marker, work row 1 of lace pat to last st, k1.
Row 6 Rep row 2.
Work even as foll:
Row 7 K1, work row 1 of lace pat to marker, sl marker, k2, work 22-st rep twice across, k3, sl marker, k5, work 22-st rep 5 times across, k4, sl marker, k3, work 22-st rep twice across, k2, sl marker, work row 1 of lace pat to last st, k1.
Cont to work charts in this way, working sts outside reps in St st and lapel sts in lace pat, through row 46 of charts.

Beg shaping
Beg with row 7, work charts with increases by working entire row of each chart as foll:
Row 7 (RS) K1, work row 1 of lace pat to marker, sl marker, work right front chart 1 to rep line, work 22-st rep twice across, work to end of chart, sl marker, work back chart 1 to rep line, work 22-st rep 5 times across, work to end of chart, sl marker, work left front chart 1 to rep line, work 22-st rep twice across, work to end of chart, sl marker, work row 1 of lace pat to last st, k1.
Cont to work charts in this way through row 45—71 sts for each front, 163 sts for back, 76 sts for each lapel.

For both sizes
Left front and lapel
Row 46 (WS) Work lace pat over left lapel sts, work in chart pat as established over left front sts to marker, cast on 18 sts for sleeve, turn—89 sts for left front. Leave rem sts on hold.

Beg chart 2
Row 1 (RS) Work chart 2 over left front sts, working 22-st rep 3 times across, work lapel sts in lace pat as established.
Cont to work pats in this way through row 36 of chart 2.

For size Large/X-Large only
Work rows 1–36 of chart 2 once more.

For both sizes
Next row (RS) Bind off 89 left front sts, work lapel sts in lace pat.
Cont in lace pat over 76 lapel sts for 29 rows more.
Next row (RS) *K2tog, k1, ssk; rep from * to last st, k1—46 sts.
Next row P1, *p2tog, p1; rep from * across—31 sts.
Bind off firmly knitwise.

Back
Row 46 (WS) Cast on 18 sts for sleeve. With WS facing, work in chart as established over 163 sts for back, cast on 18 sts at end of row—199 sts.

Beg chart 2
Row 1 (RS) Work chart 2 over back sts, working rep 8 times.
Cont to work chart in this manner through row 34 (36).

For size Large/X-Large only
Work rows 1–34 of chart 2 once more.

For both sizes
Bind off loosely knitwise.

Right front and lapel
Row 46 (WS) Cast on 18 sts for sleeve. With WS facing, work in chart as established over right front sts, work in lace pat as established to end—89 right front sts.

Beg chart 2
Row 1 (RS) Work lapel sts in lace pat as established, work chart 2 over left front sts, working rep 3 times.
Cont to work pats in this way through row 36 of chart 2.

For size Large/X-Large only
Work rows 1–36 of chart 2 once more.

For both sizes
Next row (RS) Work lapel sts in lace pat, bind off 89 left front sts. Rejoin yarn ready to work a WS row and cont in lace pat over 76 lapel sts for 29 rows more.
Next row (RS) K1, *k2tog, k1, ssk; rep from * to end—46 sts.
Next row P1, *p2tog, p1; rep from * across—31 sts.
Bind off firmly knitwise.

Finishing
Block piece lightly to measurements. Sew shoulder seams and underarm seams. Seam bound-off edges of lapels together and sew lapel to back neck edge, easing in fullness. Fold lapel to WS and sew outer edge along back neck edge between shoulder seams. Rem outer edges of lapel are not seamed.

BACK CHART 1

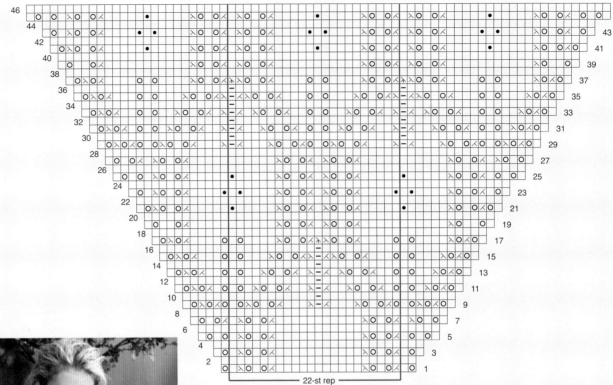

22-st rep

LEFT FRONT CHART 1

22-st rep

Lower edge

Overlap right lapel over left at lower edge and pin in place. With RS facing and shorter circular needle, pick up and k 32 sts through overlapped lapels, then pick up and k 112 (150) sts around rem of lower edge of body—144 (182) sts. Join and pm for beg of rnd.

Rnd 1 *K1, p1; rep from * around.

Rep rnd 1 for 1"/2.5cm. Bind off loosely in rib. ❖

RIGHT FRONT CHART 1

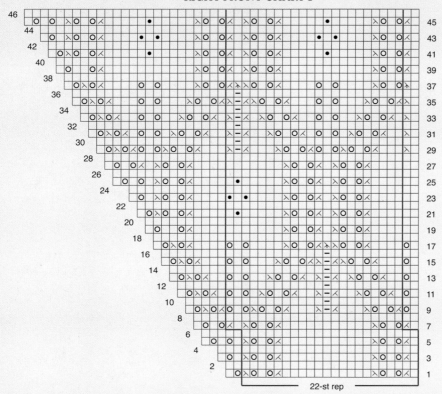

22-st rep

CHART 2

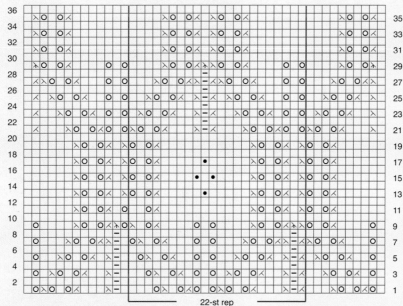

22-st rep

Stitch Key

☐ k on RS, p on WS

─ p on RS, k on WS

⊙ yo

⟋ k2tog

⟍ SKP

⌁ SK2P

● make nupp

Veil Stitch Cowl

Veil Stitch Cowl

Using a single skein and an allover mesh stitch, a drapy cowl is equally pleasurable to knit and to wear.

Designed by Hannah Wallace

Skill Level:
■■■□

Materials
- One 3½oz/100g skein (each approx 328yd/300m) of Noro *Silk Garden Sock* (wool/silk/nylon/mohair) in #349 ①
- Size 6 (4mm) circular needle, 32"/80cm long, OR SIZE TO OBTAIN GAUGE
- Stitch marker

Size
Instructions are written for one size.

Knitted Measurements
Length 13"/33cm
Circumference 72"/182.5cm

Gauge
10 sts and 12 rnds to 4"/10cm over veil st using size 6 (4mm) needle.
TAKE TIME TO CHECK GAUGE.

Veil Stitch
Insert RH needle in next st as if to knit, bring yarn to front between needles and wrap from front to back around LH needle, then between needles to back of RH needle and from back to front to back around RH needle, draw the loop of yarn that is around RH needle through the stitch only (not the extra wrap) and let the stitch and extra wrap drop from LH needle—1 st made. Rep this st for veil st.

Cowl
Cast on 180 sts. Join, being careful not to twist sts, and place marker for beg of rnd. Work in veil st until piece measures 13"/33cm from beg. Bind off in pat.

Finishing
Pin to measurements, being sure that sts are straight. Steam to block. ❖

Leaf Band Hat

Leaf Band Hat

A wide band of leafy lace and rows of eyelets on the crown lend elegance to a slouchy shape.

Designed by Cheryl Murray

Skill Level:

■■■□

Materials

- Two 1¾oz/70g skeins (each approx 109yd/100m) of Noro *Silk Garden* (silk/mohair/wool) in #373 ④
- One pair size 7 (4.5mm) needles OR SIZE TO OBTAIN GAUGE
- One set (5) size 7 (4.5mm) double-pointed needles (dpns)
- Stitch markers

Size

Instructions are written for one size, to fit adult woman.

Knitted Measurements

Head circumference 18"/45.5cm
Length 11"/28cm

Gauge

20 sts and 24 rnds to 4"/10 cm over St st using size 4 (3.5mm) needles. TAKE TIME TO CHECK GAUGE.

Hat
Band

With circular needle, cast on 17 sts.
Rep rows 1–18 of leaf chart 8 times. Bind off.
Sew cast-on edge to bound-off edge to form a tube.

Crown

With RS facing and working in back loops of each sl st, pick up and k 72 sts. Place marker (pm) for beg of rnd.
Knit 2 rnds.
Next (inc) rnd *K4, M1; rep from * around—90 sts.
Knit 4 rnds.

Begin eyelet pat
Rnd 1 Purl.
Rnd 2 *Yo, k2tog, rep from * to end.
Rnd 3 Purl.
Work 6 rnds in St st (k every rnd).
Rep last 9 rnds twice more, then rep rnds 1–3 once more.

Shape crown

Note Change to dpns when there are too few sts to fit comfortably on circular needle.
Set-up rnd *K15, pm; rep from * around.
Next (dec) rnd K to 2 sts before next marker, k2tog, sl marker; rep from * around—6 sts dec'd.
Knit 1 rnd.
Cont in St st and rep dec rnd *every other* rnd 6 times more, then *every* rnd 7 times—6 sts.
Break yarn and thread tail through open sts. Pull tight to close. ❧

LEAF CHART

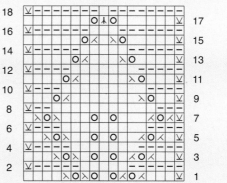

Stitch Key

□	k on RS, p on WS
─	p on RS, k on WS
⦾	yo
⋌	k2tog
⋋	SKP
⋏	S2KP
⩔	slip 1 wyib

17 sts

Tilted Blocks Scarf

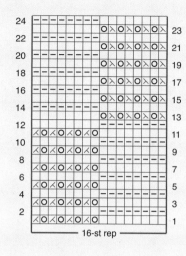

Stitch Key

- □ k on RS, p on WS
- ─ p on RS, k on WS
- ⊠ k2tog
- ⊠ ssk
- ⊙ yo

Tilted Blocks Scarf

Alternating blocks of simple lace and garter stitch naturally form a chevron pattern on a dramatic oversized scarf.

Designed by Cheryl Murray

Skill Level:
■ ■ □ □

Materials

- Four 3½oz/100g skeins (each approx 220yd/200m) of Noro *Taiyo* (cotton/silk/wool/nylon) in #35 ④
- One pair size 9 (5.5mm) needles OR SIZE TO OBTAIN GAUGE

Size

Instructions are written for one size.

Knitted Measurements

Width 21"/53.5cm
Length 72"/182.5cm

Gauge

14 sts and 24 rows to 4"/10cm over chart pat using size 9 (5.5mm) needles. TAKE TIME TO CHECK GAUGE.

Stitch Pattern

(multiple of 16 sts)
Row 1 (RS) *K8, [yo, k2tog] 4 times; rep from * to end.
Row 2 *P8, k8; rep from * to end.
Rows 3–12 Rep rows 1 and 2.
Row 13 (RS) *[Ssk, yo] 4 times, k8; rep from * to end.
Row 14 *K8, p8; rep from * to end.
Rows 15–24 Rep rows 13 and 14.
Rep rows 1–24 for stitch pat.

Note

Stitch pattern can be worked from text or chart.

Scarf

Cast on 64 sts.

Begin chart or stitch pat
Row 1 (RS) Work 16-st rep 4 times across.
Cont to work in this manner until row 24 is complete.
Rep rows 1–24 until piece measures approx 72"/182.5cm from beg, end with a row 11 or 23. Bind off loosely. ❖

Faux Cable Mitts

Faux Cable Mitts

Lace can be cozy, too, as in these fingerless mitts that feature an allover faux cable pattern.

Designed by Sandi Prosser

Skill Level:
■■■□

Materials
- One 3½oz/100g ball (each approx 220yd/201m) of Noro *Taiyo* (cotton/silk/wool/nylon) in #34 (**4**)
- One set (5) size 6 (4mm) double-pointed needles (dpns) OR SIZE TO OBTAIN GAUGE
- Stitch markers
- Scrap yarn

Size
Instructions are written for one size, to fit adult woman.

Knitted Measurements
Hand circumference 8"/20.5cm
Length 9½"/24cm

Gauge
22 sts and 29 rnds to 4"/10cm over chart pat using size 6 (4mm) needles.
TAKE TIME TO CHECK GAUGE.

P2, K2 Rib
(multiple of 4 sts)
Rnd 1 *P2, k2; rep from * to end of rnd.
Rep rnd 1 for p2, k2 rib.

Notes
1) Left and right mitts are the same.
2) Chart can be found on page 135.

Mitt
Cuff
Cast on 44 sts and divide evenly on dpns. Join, being careful not to twist sts, and place marker (pm) for beg of rnd.
Rnd 1 *P1, sl 1 purlwise wyib, k2, psso, [p2, k2] 3 times, p2, sl 1 purlwise wyif, k2, psso, p1; rep from * once more.
Rnd 2 *P1, k1, yo, k1, [p2, k2] 3 times, p2, k1, yo, k1, p1; rep from * once more.
Rnds 3 and 4 *P1, k3, [p2, k2] 3 times, p2, k3, p1; rep from * once more.
Rnd 5 Rep rnd 1.
Rnd 6 Rep rnd 2.
Rnd 7 *P1, k3, [p2, k2] 3 times, p2, k3, p1; rep from * once more.

Hand
Begin chart
Rnd 1 Work 22-st chart rep twice around.
Cont to work chart in this way until rnd 14 is complete. Rep rnds 3–12 until piece measures 5"/12.5cm from beg.

Shape thumb gusset
Next (inc) rnd M1 p-st, pm, work in pat to end of rnd—45 sts.
Next 2 rnds P1, sl marker, work in pat to end of rnd.
Next (inc) rnd M1 p-st, p1, M1 p-st, sl marker, work in pat to end of rnd—2 sts inc'd.
Next 2 rnds P3, sl marker, work in pat to end of rnd.
Cont in this way, rep inc rnd every 3rd rnd 4 times more—11 sts for thumb gusset.
Next rnd Place first 11 sts on scrap yarn for thumb, work in pat to end of rnd—44 sts. Work even in pat until piece measures 9"/23cm from beg.
Next (dec) rnd *P1, k1, k2tog, [p2, k2] 3 times, p2, k1, k2tog, p1; rep from * once more—40 sts.
Work 3 rnds in p2, k2 rib. Bind off in rib.

Thumb
Place 11 thumb sts on 3 dpns.
Rnd 1 P11, with 4th dpn, pick up and k 1 st at thumb opening—12 sts. Distribute sts evenly on 4 dpns.
Work 5 rnds in p2, k2 rib. Bind off in rib. ❧

Bobble Columns Capelet

Bobble Columns Capelet

Lace branches and bobbles form graphic columns on a garter stitch background, showing off the texture of a bulky semi-solid.

Designed by Cheryl Murray

Skill Level:

■■■□

Materials

- 5 (6) 1¾oz/50g skeins (each approx 109yd/100m) of Noro *Silk Garden Solo* (silk/mohair/wool) in #7 (5)
- One each sizes 7 and 8 (4.5 and 5mm) circular needle, 24"/60cm long, OR SIZE TO OBTAIN GAUGE
- Stitch markers

Sizes

Instructions are written for Small (Medium/Large). Shown in size Small.

Knitted Measurements

Neck circumference 24½"/62cm
Lower edge circumference 49½ (52½)"/125.5 (133)cm
Length 13 (14)"/33 (35.5)cm

Gauge

16 sts and 30 rnds to 4"/10cm over chart pat using larger needle.
TAKE TIME TO CHECK GAUGE.

Stitch Glossary

make bobble (K1, yo, k1) in next st, turn, p3, turn k3, turn, SK2P, bring working yarn to front, sl st just worked to LH needle, bring yarn to back below bobble, sl bobble st back to RH needle.

Capelet

With larger needle, cast on 198 (209) sts. Join, being careful not to twist sts, and place marker (pm) for beg of rnd.
[P 1 rnd, k 1 rnd] three times.
Next rnd P9 (10), pm, [p18 (19), pm] 10 times, p to end of rnd.

Begin chart

Rnd 1 [K to marker, sl marker, work chart rnd over next 9 sts] 11 times around.
Rnd 2 [P to marker, sl marker, work chart rnd over next 9 sts] 11 times around.
Cont to work in this manner, with panels of garter st between chart panels, until rnd 6 is complete. Rep rnds 1–6 until piece measures approx 6"/15cm from beg, end with a chart rnd 6.

For size Medium/Large only
Next (dec) rnd [K to 2 sts before marker, k2tog, sl marker, work chart rnd 1] 11 times around—198 sts.
Cont in pats as established until chart rnd 6 is complete.

For both sizes
Next (dec) rnd [Ssk, k to 2 sts before marker, k2tog, sl marker, work chart rnd 1] 11 times around—22 sts dec'd.
Cont in pats as established, rep dec rnd every 12th rnd 3 times more—110 sts.
Work even until piece measures approx 13"/33cm from beg, end with a chart rnd 6.
Change to smaller needle.
Work 7 rnds in garter st. Bind off loosely purlwise. ❖

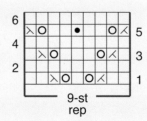

9-st rep

Stitch Key
□ k on RS, p on WS
⊙ yo
⊠ k2tog
⊠ ssk
● make bobble

Poplar Leaf Beret

Poplar Leaf Beret

Decreases within a unique leaf lace pattern help form the shape of a jaunty, feminine topper.

Designed by Patty Lyons

Skill Level:
■■■□

Materials
- Two 1¾oz/50g skeins (each approx 109yd/100m) of Noro *Silk Garden* (silk/mohair/wool) in #391 (4)
- Size 7 (4.5mm) circular needle, 16"/40cm long, OR SIZE TO OBTAIN GAUGE
- One set (5) size 7 (4.5mm) double-pointed needles
- Stitch marker

Size
Instructions are written for one size, to fit adult woman.

Knitted Measurements
Brim circumference (unstretched) 16"/40.5cm
Diameter (lying flat) 11"/28cm

Gauge
26 sts and 25 rnds to 4"/10cm over chart pat using size 7 (4.5mm) needles. TAKE TIME TO CHECK GAUGE.

Notes
1) The stitch count of the charted lace pattern changes throughout, shaping the beret.

2) Change to double-pointed needles when stitches no longer fit comfortably on circular needle.

Beret
With circular needle, cast on 72 sts. Join, being careful not to twist sts, and place marker for beg of rnd.
Next rnd *K1, p1; rep from * around.
Rep this rnd for k1, p1 rib until brim measures 1½"/4cm from beg.

Begin chart
Rnd 1 Work chart rep 6 times around.
Cont to work chart in this manner until rnd 51 is complete—12 sts.
Next rnd [K2tog] 6 times around.
Break yarn, leaving a long tail. Thread tail through rem sts and pull tight to close.

Finishing
Pin flat to diameter measurement and spray with water to block. ❖

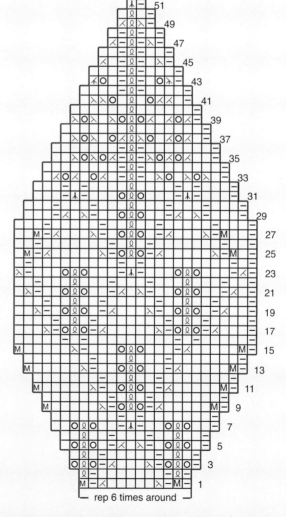

Stitch Key
- ☐ knit
- ⊟ purl
- Ⓞ yo
- Ⓠ k1tbl
- Ⓜ M1
- ╲ k2tog
- ╲ ssk
- ⊼ S2KP
- ⊼ SK2P
- ⊼ k3tog

rep 6 times around

Mitered Top

Mitered Top

Bands of color and bands of lace catch the eye on a pullover with circular-knit medallion centers.

Designed by Irina Poludnenko

Skill Level:

▣▣▣▢

Materials

- Four 1½oz/100g hanks (each approx 327yd/300m) of Noro *Silk Garden Sock* (wool/silk/polyamide/mohair) in #S84 **①**
- One set (5) size 4 (3.5mm) double-pointed needles (dpns) OR SIZE TO OBTAIN GAUGE
- One each size 4 (3.5mm) circular needles, 16, 24, and 36"/40, 60, and 92cm long
- Stitch markers, stitch holders

Sizes

Instructions are written for one size, to fit Small–X-Large.

Knitted Measurements

Bust 44"/111.5cm
Length 21"/53cm
Upper arm 14"/35.5cm

Gauge

16 sts and 30 rows/rnds to 4"/10 cm over pat st (see rows 1–10 of sleeves).

Back

Beg at the medallion center, cast on 8 sts divided evenly on 4 dpns (with 2 sts on each dpn). Join and work in rnds as foll:
Rnd 1 and all odd-numbered rnds through rnd 43 Knit.
Rnd 2 *[Yo, k1] twice; rep from * 3 times more on each of the 3 dpns.
Rnd 4 [Yo, k1, yo, ssk, yo, k1] 4 times. For the foll rnds through rnd 81 rep the stated rnd on each of the 4 dpns.
Rnd 6 Yo, k2tog, yo, k1, yo, ssk, yo, k1.
Rnd 8 Yo, k2, yo, p3tog, yo, k2, yo, k1.
Rnd 10 Yo, k1, k2tog, yo, k3, yo, ssk, k1, yo, k1.
Rnd 12 Yo, k3, yo, k1, p3tog, k1, yo, k3, yo, k1.
Rnd 14 Yo, k2, k2tog, yo, k5, yo, ssk, k2, yo, k1.
Rnd 16 Yo, k4, yo, k2, p3tog, k2, yo, k4, yo, k1.
Rnd 18 Yo, k3, k2tog, yo, k7, yo, ssk, k3, yo, k1.
Rnd 20 Yo, k5, yo, k3, p3tog, k3, yo, k5, yo, k1.
Rnd 22 Yo, k4, k2tog, yo, k9, yo, ssk, k4, yo, k1.
Rnd 24 Yo, k6, yo, k4, p3tog, k4, yo, k6, yo, k1.
Rnd 26 Yo, k5, k2tog, yo, k11, yo, ssk, k5, yo, k1.
Rnd 28 Yo, k7, yo, k5, p3tog, k5, yo, k7, yo, k1.
Rnd 30 Yo, k6, * k2tog, yo, k1, yo, ssk,* k7, rep from * to *, end k6, yo, k1.
Rnd 32 Yo, k6, * k2tog, yo, k3, yo, ssk,* k5, rep from * to *, end k6, yo, k1.
Rnd 34 [*Yo, k1, yo, ssk, k3, k2tog, yo, k1, yo*, k3tog] twice, rep from * to *, end k1.
Rnd 36 Yo, k3, yo, [ssk, k1, k2tog, yo, k3, yo, ssk, k2, yo] twice, ssk, k1, k2tog, yo, k3, yo, k1.
Rnd 38 [Yo, k1, yo, k3tog] 9 times, [yo, k1] twice.
Rnd 40 Yo, k3, [yo, ssk, k2] 9 times, yo, k1.
Rnd 42 [Yo, k1, yo, k3tog] 10 times, [yo, k1] twice.
Rnd 44 Yo, k43, yo, k1.
Rnd 45 P45, k1.
Rnd 46 Yo, p45, yo, k1.
Rnd 47 K48.
Rnd 48 Yo, k1, [yo, ssk] 23 times, yo, k1.
Rnd 49 K50.
Rnd 50 Yo, p49, yo, k1.
Rnd 51 P51, k1.
Rnd 52 Yo, k51, yo, k1.
Rnd 53 K1, [yo, ssk] 26 times, k1.
Rnd 54 Yo, k53, yo, k1.
Rnd 55 P55, k1.
Rnd 56 Yo, p55, yo, k1—232 sts.
Rnd 57 K58.
Rnd 58 Yo, k1, *yo, ssk; rep from * to last st, yo, k1.
Rnd 59 K60.
Rnd 60 Yo, p59, yo, k1.
Rnd 61 P61, k1—248 sts.
Rnd 62 Yo, k61, yo, k1.
Rnd 63 K1, *yo, ssk; rep from * to last st, k1.
Rnd 64 Yo, k63, yo, k1.

Rnd 65 P65, k1.

Rnd 66 Yo, p65, yo, k1—272 sts.

Rnd 67 K68.

Rnd 68 Rep rnd 58.

Rnd 69 K70.

Rnd 70 Yo, p69, yo, k1.

Rnd 71 P71, k1—288 sts.

Rnd 72 Yo, k71, yo, k1.

Rnd 73 Rep rnd 63.

Rnd 74 Yo, k73, yo, k1.

Rnd 75 P75, k1.

Rnd 76 Yo, p75, yo, k1—312 sts.

Rnd 77 K78.

Rnd 78 Rep rnd 58.

Rnd 79 K80.

Rnd 80 Yo, p79, yo, k1.

Rnd 81 P81, k1—328 sts.

This ends the center medallion.

Next rnd Bind off 82 sts from needle 1 (this forms the lower edge of the back), k82, place marker (pm), k82, pm, k82, turn. Purl 1 row.

Next row (RS) K81, kfb, sl marker, kfb, k80, kfb, sl marker, kfb, k81. Purl 1 row.

Next row (RS) K1 (selvage st), [k1, yo, k3tog, yo] 20 times, [k to last st before marker, kfb, sl marker, kfb] twice, [yo, k3tog, yo, k1] 20 times, k to last st, k1 (selvage st).

Purl 1 row.

Rep last 2 rows 3 times more.

Neck shaping

Next row (RS) Work to 1 st before first marker in pat as before, kfb, sl marker, kfb, k to the center 30 sts, k the 30 sts then sl these sts to a st holder (for neck), and turn.

Next row (WS) Bind off 1 st, purl to end.

Next row (RS) Work to 1 st before first marker in pat as before, kfb, sl marker, kfb, k to the neck sts, turn.

Next row (WS) Bind off 1 st, purl to end.

Rep last 2 rows once more. Bind off all sts knitwise. This completes the right seam and right shoulder of the back. Rejoin yarn after neck sts on holder and work left seam/left shoulder as for first side, reversing shaping.

Front

Work center medallion as for back.

Next rnd Bind off 82 sts from needle 1 (this forms the lower edge of the front), k82, pm, k82, pm, k82, turn. Purl 1 row.

Next row (RS) K81, (kfb) into next st, sl marker, (kfb) into next st, k34, turn, leaving rem sts on hold.

Next row (WS) Bind off 3 sts, purl to end.

Next row (RS) K1 (selvage st), [k1, yo, k3tog, yo] 20 times, k to 1 st before marker, kfb, sl marker, kfb, k to end.

Next row (WS) Bind off 2 sts, purl to end.

Rep last 2 rows 3 times more.

Next eyelet row (RS) K1 (selvage st), [k1, yo, k3tog, yo] 20 times, k to 1 st before marker, kfb, sl marker, kfb, k to end.

Next row (WS) Bind off 1 st, purl to end.

Next row (RS) Rep eyelet row.

Next row Purl.

Rep the last 2 rows twice more. Bind off all sts knitwise.

To work opposite side of neck, first sl the center 12 sts to a st holder. Then, rejoin yarn after these sts and work 2nd side of neck shaping as for front, reversing shaping.

Sleeves

Cast on 50 sts.

Row 1 Purl.

Rows 2 and 3 Knit.

Row 4 K1, *yo, p2tog; rep from *, end k1.

Rows 5 and 6 Knit.

Rows 7 and 8 Purl.

Row 9 K1, *k2tog, yo; rep from *, end k1.

Row 10 Purl.

Rep rows 1–10 for pat st, inc 1 st each side every 10th row 4 times—58 sts. When there are a total of 13 reps of the 10-row pat, work 2 rows in reverse St st and bind off.

Finishing

Sew shoulder seams.

Neckband

From the RS, using shorter circular needle, pick up and k 88 sts around the neck edge, including sts from holders. Join and pm to mark beg of rnd.

Purl 2 rnds, knit 1 rnd.

Next rnd *Yo, k2tog; rep from * around. Knit 1 rnd, purl 2 rnds. Bind off knitwise. Fold sleeves in half and sew to side seams of piece with the fold matching the shoulder seam. Sew side and sleeve seam.

Lower edge trim

With larger circular needle, pick up and k 222 sts around lower edge. Join and pm to mark beg of rnd. Purl 2 rnds, k1 rnd.

Next rnd *Yo, k2tog; rep from * around. Knit 1 rnd, purl 2 rnds. Bind off knitwise. ❖

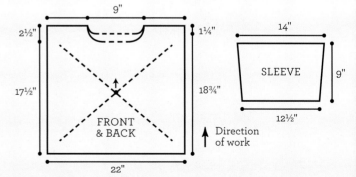

Buttoned Wrap

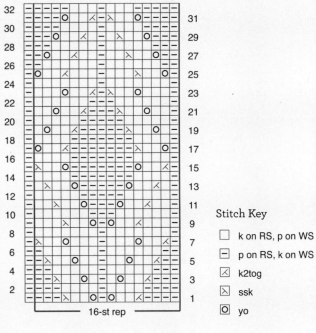

Stitch Key

- ☐ k on RS, p on WS
- ⊟ p on RS, k on WS
- ☒ k2tog
- ⊠ ssk
- ◉ yo

Buttoned Wrap

A rectangle covered in wave lace that buttons to form a diagonal wrap exudes luxe style.

Designed by Wei Wilkins

Skill Level:

■■■☐

Materials

- 5 (5, 6) 1¾oz/50g hanks (each approx 196yd/180m) of Noro *Shiraito* (cashmere/angora/wool) in #21 ❶
- One pair each sizes 4 and 5 (3.5 and 3.75mm) needles OR SIZE TO OBTAIN GAUGE
- Seven ¾"/19mm buttons

Sizes

Instructions are written for Small (Medium, Large). Shown in size Small.

Knitted Measurements

Width 16"/40.5cm
Length 48 (50, 52)"/122 (127, 132)cm

Gauge

24 sts and 30 rows to 4"/10cm over chart pat using larger needles. TAKE TIME TO CHECK GAUGE.

Wrap

With smaller needles, cast on 97 sts. Knit 12 rows. Change to larger needles.

Begin chart

Row 1 (RS) K8, work 16-st rep 5 times across, k to end of chart, k8.
Row 2 K8, work to rep line, work 16-st rep 5 times across, k8.
Cont to work chart in this manner until row 32 is complete. Rep rows 1–32 until piece measures approx 47 (49, 51)"/119.5 (124.5, 129.5)cm from beg, end with a chart row 16 or 32.
Change to smaller needles. Knit 6 rows.
Next (buttonhole) row (RS) K4, bind off 2 sts, [k13, bind off 2 sts, k12, bind off 2 sts] 3 times, k4.
Next row Knit, casting on 2 sts over each set of bound-off sts. Knit 4 rows. Bind off.

Finishing

Using photo as guide, sew buttons to correspond to buttonholes. ❖

Infinity Scarf

Infinity Scarf

The mesh borders of a drapey, circular-knit infinity scarf are cleverly designed to match using a provisional cast-on.

Designed by Angela Tong

Skill Level:

■■■□

Materials

- One 3½oz/100g skeins (each approx 462yd/420m) of Noro *Taiyo Sock* (cotton/wool/nylon/silk) in #S49 **1**
- Size 7 (4.5mm) circular needle, 40"/100cm long, OR SIZE TO OBTAIN GAUGE
- Size 7 (4.5mm) crochet hook
- Size 8 (5mm) knitting needle for binding off
- Scrap yarn
- Stitch marker

Size

Instructions are written for one size.

Knitted Measurements

Circumference 66"/167.5cm
Length 5½"/14cm

Gauge

18 sts and 31 rnds to 4"/10cm after blocking over lace rib using size 7 (4.5mm) needle. TAKE TIME TO CHECK GAUGE.

Provisional Cast-On

With scrap yarn and crochet hook, ch the number of sts to cast on plus a few extra. Cut a tail and pull the tail through the last chain. With knitting needle and yarn, pick up and k the stated number of sts through the "purl bumps" on the back of the chain. To remove scrap chain, when instructed, pull out the tail from the last crochet stitch. Gently and slowly pull on the tail to unravel the crochet stitches, carefully placing each released knit stitch on a needle.

K2, P2 Rib

Rnd 1 *K2, p2; rep from * around.
Rep rnd 1 for k2, p2 rib.

Lace Rib

(multiple of 4 sts)
Rnd 1 *K2tog, yo, p2; rep from * around.
Rnd 2 *K2, p2; rep from * around.
Rnd 3 *Yo, SKP, p2; rep from * around.
Rnd 4 Rep rnd 2.
Rep rows 1–4 for lace rib.

Cowl

Cast on 300 sts using provisional cast-on method. Join, being careful not to twist sts, and place marker for beg of rnd.
Work 6 rnds in k2, p2 rib.

Begin lace rib

Work rnds 1–4 of lace rib 4 times.
Work 5 rnds in k2, p2 rib.

Begin mesh border

Rnd 1 *Yo, k2tog; rep from * around.
Rnd 2 Knit.
Rnd 3 *SKP, yo; rep from * around.
Rnd 4 Knit.
Rnd 5 Purl.
Bind off as foll: With larger needle, k1, sl st back to LH needle, *k2tog, sl st back to LH needle; rep from * until 1 st rem. Fasten off.

Second border

Carefully remove scrap yarn from provisional cast-on and place 300 sts on circular needle. Work mesh border and bind off as for opposite edge.

Finishing

Soak cowl and pin to measurements to block. ❖

Square Shrug

Square Shrug

Geometry equals drama in an oversize shrug constructed from a lacy medallion worked from the center out, folded, and seamed.

Designed by Wei Wilkins

Skill Level:
■■■■

Materials

- Four 3½oz/100g skeins (each approx 457d/420m) of Noro *Taiyo Sock* (cotton/wool/nylon/silk) in #S8 (1)
- One set (5) size 4 (3.5mm) double-pointed needles (dpns) OR SIZE TO OBTAIN GAUGE
- One each size 4 (3.5mm) circular needles, 24 and 40"/60 and 100cm long
- Stitch markers

Size
Instructions are written for one size.

Knitted Measurements
Width 42"/106.5cm
Length 21¼"/54.5cm

Gauge
24 sts and 36 rnds to 4"/10cm over 10-st/16-row pat rep using size 4 (3.5mm) needles. TAKE TIME TO CHECK GAUGE.

Notes
1) Yo incs are worked every other rnd at the beg and end of each of the 4 rep sections as indicated in chart and cont throughout piece when chart is complete.
2) When working inc'd sts into 10-st/16-row pat rep, take care to work yos *only* when there are enough sts to work the corresponding dec, and do not work a dec without a corresponding yo.
3) Change to circular needle when necessary and place markers to mark the 4 sections.
4) Chart can be found on page 136.

Shrug
With dpn, cast on 8 sts and divide evenly on 4 dpns. Join, being careful not to twist sts, and place marker for beg of rnd.
Knit 1 rnd.

Begin chart
Next rnd Work rnd 1 of chart 4 times around—8 sts inc'd.
Cont in this manner until rnd 44 is complete—184 sts.
Cont in pat as established, working inc'd sts into pat rep (see notes), until 188 rows have been worked in pat (piece measures approx 21"/53.5cm from center to edge, measured at center of rep section), end with a knit rnd—760 sts.

Finishing
Next rnd Bind off 190 sts for side, p190 and place on spare needle to hold for lower edge, bind off 190 sts for side, p190 and place on hold for lower edge.

Armholes
Fold piece in half so that the lower edges are tog. Place markers 8"/20.5cm down from fold on front and back of both sides.
Sew seams from lower edge to markers.

Trim
Place open sts on longer circular needle. Work 4 rnds garter st (k 1 rnd, p 1 rnd). Bind off. ❖

Loop Mesh Scarf

Loop Mesh Scarf

A unique fabric of interlocking loops formed with short rows makes a head-turning statement scarf.

Designed by Amanda Blair Brown

Skill Level:
■■■□

Materials
- Three 3½oz/100g skeins (each approx 327yd/300m) of Noro *Silk Garden Sock* (wool/silk/polyamide/mohair) in #58 **1**
- One pair size 6 (4mm) needles OR SIZE TO OBTAIN GAUGE

Size
Instructions are written for one size.

Knitted Measurements
Width (unstretched) 6"/15cm
Length 70"/177.5cm

Gauges
33 sts and 16 rows to 4"/10cm over pat st using size 6 (4mm) needles.
21 sts and 24 rows to 4"/10cm over St st using size 6 (4mm) needles.
TAKE TIME TO CHECK GAUGES.

Pattern Stitch
(multiple of 8 sts plus 2)
Row 1 K4, [turn, sl 1 purlwise, p3, turn, k4] 7 times, [k8, *turn, sl 1 purlwise, p5, turn, sl 1 purlwise, k5; rep from * 6 times more] 5 times, k6, [turn, p4, turn, sl 1 purlwise, k3] 7 times.
Row 2 Purl.
Row 3 Knit.m
Row 4 Purl.
Row 5 (RS) [K8, *turn, sl 1 purlwise, p5, turn, sl 1 purlwise, k5; rep from * 6 times more] 6 times, k2.
Rows 6–8 Rep rows 2–4.
Rep rows 1–8 for pat st.

Scarf
Cast on 50 sts. Work in pat st until piece measures approx 70"/177.5cm, end with a row 3. Bind off. ❖

Short Row Shawl

Short Row Shawl

Short rows create a curve that sweeps around the shoulders and gives subtle shape to bands of stockinette and mesh lace.

Designed by Charles Voth

Skill Level:
■■■■

Materials
- Two 3½oz/100g skeins (each approx 328yd/300m) of Noro *Silk Garden Sock* (wool/silk/polyamide/mohair) in #272 ①
- One pair size 5 (3.75.mm) needles OR SIZE TO OBTAIN GAUGE
- Stitch markers

Size
Instructions are written for one size.

Knitted Measurements
Width at widest point 19"/48cm
Wingspan approx 46"/116cm

Gauge
17 sts and 24 rows to 4"/10cm over St st using size 5 (3.75mm) needles. TAKE TIME TO CHECK GAUGE.

Stitch Glossary
wrapped bind-off (wbo) P1, *yo, purl next st, pass yo and previous st over st just purled; rep from * until all sts are bound off.
lift back bar (lbb) Insert LH needle under bar at back of horizontal bound-off st in previous row and knit it.

Short Row Wrapping (wrap and turn—w&t)
1) Wyib, sl next st purlwise.
2) Move yarn between the needles to the front (back).
3) Sl the same st back to LH needle. Turn work, bring yarn to the knit (purl) side between needles. One st is wrapped.

Note
When working horizontal row 2, there are 2 fewer sts to pick up than the number of sts bound off in the previous row. Incs are worked to compensate. When horizontal row 2 is complete, the st count will be the same as before working horizontal row 1.

Shawl
Cast on 32 sts. Knit 3 rows.
Horizontal row 1 (WS) P2, sl 1, wbo to last 3 sts, p2.
Horizontal row 2 (RS) K2, M1L, lbb in each bound-off st, M1L, k2.
Purl 1 row.
Next row (RS) K2, *yo, k2tog; rep from * to last 2 sts, k2.
Purl 1 row.
Short row 1 (RS) K2, *yo, k2tog; rep from * to last 12 sts, k1, w&t, sl 1, p to end.
Short row 2 (RS) K2, *yo, k2tog, rep from * to 2 sts before last wrapped st, w&t, sl 1, p to end.
Next row (RS) Knit.
Work horizontal rows 1 and 2.
**Next row (WS) P to last 10 sts, place marker (pm), p to end.

Increase band
Next (inc) row (RS) K to marker, M1L, sl marker, k to last 12 sts, M1L, k to end.

Cont in St st and rep inc row every other row 4 times more—10 sts inc'd.
Work horizontal rows 1 and 2.

Short row lace band
Short row 1 (RS) K2, *yo, k2tog; rep from * to last 12 sts, k1, w&t, sl 1, p to end.
Short row 2 (RS) K2, *yo, k2tog, rep from * to 2 sts before last wrapped st, w&t, sl 1, p to end.
Rep short row 2 until 11 sts rem unwrapped.
Knit 1 row.
Work horizontal rows 1 and 2.
Rep from ** 5 times more, placing marker for inc band 5 sts farther from end of WS row each time—92 sts.
Next row (WS) P to last 36 sts, pm, p to end.

***Decrease band
Next (dec) row (RS) K to marker, sl marker, ssk, k to last 16 sts, ssk, k to end.
Cont in St st and rep dec row every other row 4 times more—10 sts dec'd.
Work horizontal rows 1 and 2.

Short row lace band
Short row 1 (RS) K2, *yo, k2tog; rep from * to last 12 sts, k1, w&t, sl 1, p to end.
Short row 2 (RS) K2, *yo, k2tog, rep from * to 2 sts before last wrapped st, w&t, sl 1, p to end.
Rep short row 2 until last WS row is *sl 1, p10*.
Knit 1 row.
Work horizontal rows 1 and 2.
Rep from *** 5 times more—32 sts.
Purl 3 rows. Bind off.

Finishing
With crochet hook, join yarn to any corner with sl st, always working under 2 strands of yarn when inserting hook, work evenly around entire edge of shawl as foll: *Ch 5, insert hook in next edge st, yo, pull up loop, yo, pull through 2 loops, sk 2 or 3 edge sts, insert hook in next edge st, yo, pull up loop, yo, pull through all loops on hook; rep from * around. Fasten off. ✤

Gauntlet Mitts

Gauntlet Mitts

Extended lace cuffs with a scalloped edge create a uniquely delicate gauntlet shape.

Designed by Debbie O'Neill

Skill Level:
■■■□

Materials
- Two 1¾oz/50g skeins (each approx 109yd/100m) of Noro *Silk Garden* (silk/mohair/wool) in #387 (4)
- One set (5) size 4 (3.5mm) double-pointed needles (dpns) OR SIZE TO OBTAIN GAUGE
- Stitch markers
- Scrap yarn

Size
Instructions are written for one size, to fit adult woman.

Knitted Measurements
Hand circumference 8"/20.5cm
Length 9"/23cm

Gauge
17 sts and 28 rnds to 4"/10cm over St st using size 4 (3.5mm) needles. TAKE TIME TO CHECK GAUGE.

Lace Pattern
(multiple of 10 sts)
Rnd 1 *K2tog, k4, yo, k1, yo, ssk, k1; rep from * around.
Rnd 2 and all even-numbered rnds Knit.
Rnd 3 *K2tog, k3, yo, k1, yo, k1, ssk, k1; rep from * around.
Rnd 5 *K2tog, k2, yo, k1, yo, k2, ssk, k1; rep from * around.
Rnd 7 *K2tog, k1, yo, k1, yo, k3, ssk, k1; rep from * around.
Rnd 8 Knit.
Rep rnds 1–8 for lace pat.

Note
Lace pat may be worked from chart or text.

Right Mitt
Cast on 40 sts. Join, being careful not to twist sts, and place marker (pm) for beg of rnd.

Begin lace pat or chart
Rnd 1 Work 10-st rep of lace pat 4 times around.
Cont to work in this manner until rnd 8 is complete. Rep rnds 1–8 twice more.
Knit 3 rnds.
Next rnd Knit, dec 6 sts evenly around—34 sts.
Knit 2 rnds.

Shape thumb gusset
Next rnd K to last 18 sts, pm, M1, k1, M1 pm, k to end of rnd—36 sts.
Knit 1 rnd.
Next (inc) rnd K to marker, sl marker, M1, k to marker, M1, sl marker, k to end of rnd—2 sts inc'd.
Rep inc rnd every other rnd 4 times more—13 sts between gusset markers.
Next rnd K to first marker, place next 13 sts on scrap yarn for thumb, cast on 3 sts, k to end of rnd—36 sts.
Cont in St st until piece measures 8½"/21.5cm from beg.
Next (dec) rnd *K4, k2tog; rep from * around—30 sts.
Next rnd *K2, p2; rep from * around.
Bind off in pat.

Left Mitt
Work as for right mitt to shape thumb gusset.
Next rnd K7, pm, M1, k1, M1, pm, k to end of rnd—36 sts.
Complete as for right mitt. ❧

LACE PATTERN

Stitch Key
□ knit
⊠ k2tog
⊠ ssk
Ⓞ yo

10-st rep

Long & Leafy Cowl

Long & Leafy Cowl

A cowl that can be worn wrapped snugly or with a loose drape features a classic leaf lace pattern.

Designed by Ellen Liguori

Skill Level:

■■■□

Materials

- Five 1¾oz/50g skeins (each approx 109yd/100m) of Noro *Silk Garden* (silk/mohair/wool) in #389 (4)
- One pair size 8 (5mm) needles OR SIZE TO OBTAIN GAUGE

Size

Instructions are written for one size.

Knitted Measurements

Width (unstretched) 9"/23cm
Circumference 70"/177.5cm

Gauge

20 sts and 23 rows to 4"/10cm over chart pat using size 8 (5mm) needles. TAKE TIME TO CHECK GAUGE.

Cowl

Cast on 42 sts.

Begin chart

Row 1 (RS) K3, p1, work chart row to rep line, work 10-st rep 3 times across, work to end of chart, p1, k3.
Row 2 K1, p2, k1, work chart row to rep line, work 10-st rep 3 times across, work to end of chart, k1, p2, k1.
Cont to work chart in this manner until row 26 is complete. Rep rows 1–26 until piece measures 70"/177.5cm from beg.
Bind off.

Finishing

Sew cast-on edge to bound-off edge. ❖

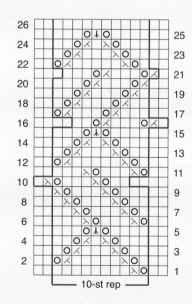

Stitch Key

- ☐ k on RS, p on WS
- ○ yo
- ⟋ k2tog on RS, p2tog on WS
- ⟍ SKP on RS, p2tog tbl on WS
- ⅄ S2KP

10-st rep

Ruffle-Edge Scarf

Ruffle-Edge Scarf

A soft and dense mesh pattern flows into a double ruffle at each end for a bit of feminine flair.

Designed by Lisa Craig

Skill Level:

■■■■

Materials

■ Two 3½oz/100g skeins (each approx 350yd/320m) of Noro *Taiyo Sport* (cotton/wool/silk) in #3 🔲③

■ Two pairs size 6 (4mm) needles OR SIZE TO OBTAIN GAUGE

Sizes

Instructions are written for one size.

Knitted Measurements

Width 6"/15.5cm
Length 50"/127cm

Gauge

22 sts and 30 rows to 4"/10cm over garter st using size 6 (4mm) needles. TAKE TIME TO CHECK GAUGE.

Diamond Pattern

(multiple of 16 sts plus 10)
Row 1 (RS) K12, k2tog, yo, *k14, k2tog, yo; rep from * to last 12 sts, k12.
Row 2 and all WS rows Knit.
Row 3 *K4, k2tog, yo, k5, k2tog, yo, k1, yo, k2tog; rep from * to last 10 sts, k4, k2tog, yo, k4.
Row 5 K3, *k2tog, yo, k1, yo, k2tog, k2, k2tog, yo, k3, yo, k2tog, k2; rep from * to last 7 sts, k2tog, yo, k1, yo, k2tog, k2.
Row 7 K2, *k2tog, yo, k3, yo, [k2tog] twice, yo, k5, yo, k2tog; rep from * to last 8 sts, k2tog, yo, k3, yo, k2tog, k1.
Row 9 *K4, yo, SK2P, yo, k4, yo, k2tog, k1, k2tog, yo; rep from * to last 10 sts, k4, yo, SK2P, yo, k3.
Row 11 K4, *k2tog, yo, k6, yo, SK2P, yo, k5; rep from * to last 6 sts, k2tog, yo, k4.
Row 13 K12, *k2tog, yo, k14; rep from * to last 14 sts, k2tog, yo, k12.
Row 14 Knit.
Work rows 1–14 for diamond pat.

Mesh Pattern

(multiple of 4 sts plus 2)
Row 1 (RS) K1, *k2, (yo twice), k2; rep from * to last st, k1.
Row 2 K1, *p2tog, (k1, p1) in double yo, p2tog, rep from * to last st, k1.
Row 3 K1, *k4, (yo twice); rep from * to last 5 sts, k5.
Row 4 K1, p2, *p2tog, (k1, p1) in double yo, p2tog; rep from * to last 3 sts, p2, k1.
Rep rows 1–4 for mesh pat.

Scarf
Small ruffle (make 2)

Cast on 58 sts.
Knit 2 rows.
Next (eyelet) row (RS) K1, *k2tog, yo; rep from * to last st, k1.
Next row Knit.
Next row K2, p to last 2 sts, k2.
Rep last 2 rows 4 times more.
Next (dec) row K1, *k2tog; rep from * to last st, k1—30 sts.
Next row K2, p to last 2 sts, k2.
Set work aside.

Diamond Ruffle

Cast on 58 sts.

Knit 2 rows.

Next (eyelet) row (RS) K1, *k2tog, yo; rep from * to last st, k1.

Knit 7 rows.

Work rows 1–14 of diamond pat.

Knit 28 rows.

Next (dec) row (RS) K1, *k2tog; rep from * to last 2 sts, k1—30 sts.

Knit 1 row.

Join first small ruffle

With RS facing, place small ruffle in front of diamond ruffle.

Next (joining) row (RS) *K first st of small ruffle tog with first st of diamond ruffle; rep from * until all sts are joined.

Purl 1 row.

Knit 4 rows.

Next (eyelet) row (RS) K1, *k2tog, yo; rep from * to last st, k1.

Knit 4 rows.

Purl 1 row.

Begin mesh pat

Work in mesh pat until scarf measures 46"/117cm from beg, end with a row 4.

Knit 1 row, purl 1 row.

Knit 4 rows.

Next (eyelet) row (RS) K1, *k2tog, yo; rep from * to last st, k1.

Knit 4 rows.

Purl 1 row.

Join 2nd small ruffle

Place small ruffle in front of work with RS tog. Join as for first small ruffle.

Knit 1 row.

Next row (RS) K1, *kfb; rep from * across, k1—58 sts.

Knit 28 rows.

Begin diamond pat

Work the 14 rows of diamond pat.

Knit 6 rows.

Next (eyelet) row (RS) K1, *k2tog, yo; rep from * to last st, k1.

Knit 2 rows.

Bind off purlwise. ❖

Circular Shawl

Circular Shawl

Lace comes full circle in a show-stopping shawl worked from the center out with a knitted-on edging.

Designed by Marin Melchior

Skill Level:

■■■■

Materials

- Seven 1³⁄₄oz/50g hanks (each approx 196yd/180m) of Noro *Shiraito* (silk/mohair/wool) in #18 ❶
- Size 7 (5.5mm) circular needle, 16"/40cm long
- Size 9 (4.5mm) circular needle, 36"/80cm long, OR SIZE TO OBTAIN GAUGE
- One set (5) size 5 (3.75mm) double-pointed needles (dpns)
- One size 9 (5.5mm) double-pointed needle for edging
- Stitch marker
- Crochet hook and scrap yarn

Sizes

Instructions are written for one size.

Knitted Measurements

Diameter including edging 53"/134.5cm

Gauge

18 sts and 24 rows to 4"/10cm over St st using size 9 (5.5mm) needles. TAKE TIME TO CHECK GAUGE.

Stitch Glossary

kfbf Knit into the front, back, front of next st to inc 2 sts.

Provisional Cast-On

With scrap yarn and crochet hook, ch the number of sts to cast on plus a few extra. Cut a tail and pull the tail through the last chain. With knitting needle and yarn, pick up and knit the stated number of sts through the "purl bumps" on the back of the chain. To remove scrap yarn chain, when instructed, pull out the tail from the last crochet stitch. Gently and slowly pull on the tail to unravel the crochet stitches, carefully placing each released knit stitch on a needle.

Notes

1) Stitch count of pattern rep changes from row to row.

2) Move beg-of-rnd marker at ends of rnds where indicated in chart.

3) Charts can be found on page 137.

Shawl

With smaller dpns, cast on 9 sts. Join, being careful not to twist sts, and place marker for beg of round.
Knit 1 rnd.
Next (inc) rnd *Yo, k1; rep from * around—18 sts.
Next rnd Knit, working yos tbl.
Knit 2 rnds.
Next (inc) rnd *Yo, k1; rep from * around—36 sts.
Next rnd Knit, working yos tbl.
Knit 5 rnds.
Next (inc) rnd *Yo, k1; rep from * around—72 sts.
Next rnd Knit, working yos tbl.

Begin chart 1

Rnd 1 Work 12-st rep 6 times around.
Cont to work chart in this manner until rnd 11 is complete.
Next (inc) rnd *Yo, k1; rep from * around—144 sts.
Knit 1 rnd.
Change to smaller circular needle. Knit 1 rnd.

Begin chart 2

Rnd 1 Work 12-st rep 12 times around.

Cont to work chart in this manner until rnd 24 is complete.

Next (inc) rnd *Yo, k1; rep from * around—288 sts.

Knit 1 rnd.

Change to larger circular needle.

Rep rounds 1–24 of chart 2 twice more.

Next (inc) rnd *Yo, k1; rep from * around—576 sts.

Knit 1 rnd.

Rep rnds 1–24 of chart 2 once more, then rep rnds 1–12 once more.

Knit 1 rnd, purl 1 rnd, knit 1 rnd. Break yarn, leaving a long tail.

Edging

With larger dpn, cast on 12 sts, using provisional cast-on method.

Next (set-up) row (RS) K11, k2tog (1 st from edging with 1 st from shawl).

Note Work the k2tog at beg of WS rows and end of RS row using 1 edging st and 1 st from shawl.

Row 1 (WS) K2tog, k2, yo, k2tog, k2, yo, k2tog, yo, k3.

Row 2 (RS) K3, yo, k2tog, yo, k5, yo, k2tog, k2tog.

Row 3 (WS) K2tog, k2, yo, k2tog, k4, yo, k2tog, yo, k3.

Row 4 (RS) K3, yo, k2tog, yo, k7, yo, k2tog, k2tog (1 st from edging with 1 st from shawl).

Row 5 (WS) K2tog, k2, yo, k2tog, k6, yo, k2tog, yo, k3.

Short row 6 (RS) K3, turn, k3.

Row 7 (RS) K3, yo, k2tog, yo, k2, k2tog, yo, k1, yo, k2tog, k2, yo, k2tog, k2tog.

Row 8 (WS) K2tog, k2, yo, k2tog, k1, yo, SK2P, yo, k4, yo, k2tog, yo, k3.

Row 9 (RS) K2, [k2tog, yo] twice, k2tog, k1, k2tog, yo, k1, yo, k2tog, k2, yo, k2tog, k2tog.

Row 10 (WS) K2tog, k2, yo, k2tog, k5, [k2tog, yo] twice, k2tog, k2.

Short row 11 (RS) K2, k2tog, turn, k3.

Row 12 (RS) K3, [yo, k2tog] twice, k6, yo, k2tog, k2tog.

Row 13 (WS) K2tog, k2, yo, k2tog, k3, k2tog, [yo, k2tog] twice, k2.

Row 14 (RS) K2, [k2tog, yo] twice, k2tog, k4, yo, k2tog, k2tog.

Row 15 (WS) K2tog, k2, yo, k2tog, k1, [K2tog, yo] twice, k2tog, k2.

Row 16 (RS) K2, [k2tog, yo] twice, k2tog, k2, yo, k2tog, k2tog.

Rep rows 1–16 until 2 shawl sts rem unjoined. Work next edging row beg with k3tog instead of k2tog.

Remove scrap yarn from provisional cast-on and graft beg and end of edging tog, using Kitchener st. ❖

Leather-Trimmed Tote

Leather-Trimmed Tote

Hard and soft achieve harmony in an oversize tote with leather lacing at the top, a fabric lining, and bamboo handles.

Designed by Fran Gross

Skill Level:

■■■□

Materials

- Five 1¾oz/50g skeins (each approx 109yd/100m) of Noro *Kureyon* (wool) in #40 (4)
- One pair each sizes 8 and 10 (5.5 and 6mm) needles OR SIZE TO OBTAIN GAUGE
- 1yd/1m lining fabric
- Two 10"/25cm bamboo ring handles
- Sewing needle and thread to match fabric
- Approx 7 large beads to embellish leather ends

Knitted Measurements

Width at lower edge 17½"/44.5cm
Length not including handles 17"/43cm

Gauge

16 sts and 21 rows to 4"/10cm over chart pat using A and smaller needles. TAKE TIME TO CHECK GAUGE.

Note

Chart can be found on page 137.

Back

With smaller needles and A, cast on 69 sts.

Begin chart

Row 1 (RS) Work 23-st rep 3 times across.
Cont to work chart in this manner until row 10 is complete. Rep rows 1–10 for 8 times more.
Next (dec) row (RS) [K4, k2tog] 11 times, k3—58 sts.
Change to larger needles and B.
Next (dec) row (WS) [K3, k2tog] 11 times, k3—47 sts.
Cont in rev St st (p on RS, k on WS) for 1½"/4cm, end with a WS row.
Next (dec) row (RS) [P3, p2tog] 9 times, p to end—38 sts.
Work 3 rows even.
Next (dec) row (RS) [P3, p2tog] 7 times, p to end—31 sts.
Work 3 rows even.
Next (dec) row (RS) [P3, p2tog] 6 times, p1—25 sts.
Work even until piece measures 6"/15cm from beg of leather section.
Bind off. Break yarn, leaving a long tail for sewing channel for handle.

Front

Work as for back.

Finishing

Block wool portions of front and back to open lace.

Lining

Place lining fabric on wool portion of back and trace the shape. Cut 2 pieces, leaving a ½"/1.5cm seam allowance all around.
Sew lining seams, leaving top open. Sew seams of wool portions of tote and weave in all wool ends. Place lining in tote and sew upper edge of lining to top row of wool portion of tote.

Handles

Place handle on WS of top edge of leather portion of tote. Fold edge around handle to form a channel and sew handle into channel using the bound-off leather tail.
Rep for other handle. Sew leather side seams.

Leather embellishment

Cut 3 strands of leather lacing approx 16"/40.5cm long. Weave into leather portion of tote at upper edge of side seam. Tie a knot on the RS of tote and thread a bead through all 3 strands to just below the knot. Braid the 3 strands tog for approx 3"/7.5cm and place another bead below the braid. Add beads to strands as desired and knot the ends. ❖

Floral Pointed Scarf

Floral Pointed Scarf

A delicate floral lace pattern and gradual narrowing toward the ends create a lighter-than-air piece of neckwear.

Designed by Mari Tobita

Skill Level:

■■■□

Materials

- One 3½oz/100g skein (each approx 918yd/840m) of Noro *Taiyo Lace* (cotton/wool/polyamide/silk) in #57 🔟
- One pair size 5 (3.75mm) needles OR SIZE TO OBTAIN GAUGE
- Spare needle
- Tapestry needle (for Kitchener st)

Knitted Measurements

Width at widest point 11"/28cm
Length 60"/152.5cm

Gauge

28 sts and 37 rows to 4"/10cm after blocking over chart 3 pat using size 5 (3.75mm) needles. TAKE TIME TO CHECK GAUGE.

Notes

1) Scarf is worked in 2 pieces and joined in the center using Kitchener stitch.
2) Charts can be found on pages 138–139.

Left Side

Cast on 4 sts. Knit 3 rows.
Next (inc) row (RS) K to last 3 sts, M1, k to end—1 st inc'd.
Cont in garter st (k every row) and rep inc row every other row twice more—7 sts. Knit 2 rows.

Begin chart 1

Work rows 1–28 of chart 1—19 sts.

Begin chart 2

Work rows 1–20 of chart 2—27 sts.
Next row (RS) Work row 1 of chart 2 to rep line, work 8-st rep twice across, work to end of chart.
Cont to work chart 2 in this way until row 20 is complete.
Rep rows 1–20 five times more, adding 1 additional 8-st rep each time the 20 rows are complete. Then rep rows 1–4 once more—76 sts.

Begin chart 3

Row 1 (RS) Work row 1 of chart 3 to rep line, work 8-st rep 7 times across, work to end of row.
Cont to work chart 3 in this way until row 20 is complete. Rep rows 1–20 four times more, adding 1 additional 8-st rep each time the 20 rows are complete. Then, rep rows 1–16 once.
Place sts on spare needle to hold.

Right Side

Cast on 4 sts. Knit 2 rows.
Next (inc) row (RS) K3, M1, k to end—1 st inc'd.
Cont in garter st and rep inc row every other row twice more—7 sts.

Begin chart 4

Work rows 1–38 of chart 4—23 sts.

Begin chart 5

Work rows 1–20 of chart 5—31 sts.
Next row (RS) Work row 1 of chart 5 to rep line, work 8-st rep twice across, work to end of chart. Cont to work chart in this way until row 20 is complete. Rep row 1–20 four times more, working 1 additional 8-st rep each time the 20 rows are complete. Then, rep rows 1–14 once—76 sts.

Begin chart 6

Row 1 (RS) Work to rep line, work 8-st rep 7 times across, work to end of chart.
Cont to work chart 6 in this way until row 20 is complete. Rep rows 1–20 three times more, adding 1 additional 8-st rep each time the 20 rows are complete. Then, rep rows 1–17.

Finishing

Graft the 2 sides tog using Kitchener st. ❖

Elbow-Length Gloves

Elbow-Length Gloves

A lace panel along the back emphasizes the long lines of a dramatic pair of gloves.

Designed by Pat Olski

Skill Level:

■■■■

Materials
- Two 1¾oz/100g skeins (each approx 197yd/180m) of Noro *Shiraito* (cashmere/angora/wool) in #34 ❶
- One set (5) each sizes 2 and 3 (2.75 and 3.25mm) double-pointed needles (dpns) OR SIZE TO OBTAIN GAUGE
- Stitch markers
- Cable needle (cn)
- Scrap yarn

Size
Instructions are written for one size, to fit adult woman.

Knitted Measurements
Wrist circumference 7"/18cm
Length 14"/35.5cm

Gauge
26 sts and 36 rnds to 4"/10cm over St st using size smaller needles.
TAKE TIME TO CHECK GAUGE.

Stitch Glossary
2-st RC Sl 1 st to cn and hold to *back*, k1, k1 from cn.
2-st LC Sl 1 st to cn and hold to *front*, k1, k1 from cn.
3-st RC Sl 2 sts to cn and hold to *back*, k1, k2 from cn.

K1, P1 Rib
(over an even number of sts)
Rnd 1 *K1, p1; rep from * around.
Rep rnd 1 for k1, p1 rib.

Left Glove
With larger needles, cast on 48 sts. Join, being careful not to twist sts, and place marker (pm) for beg of rnd.
Work in k1, p1 rib for 9 rnds.

Begin chart
Rnd 1 Work chart pat over 25 sts, pm for palm, k to end of rnd.
Cont to work chart in this manner, slipping markers every rnd, until rnd 19 is complete.
Change to smaller needles.
Rep rnds 1–19 once more, then rnds 1–8.
Next rnd Work to marker, sl marker, work in k1, p1 rib to end of rnd.
Cont in this manner until rnd 16 is complete.
Next rnd Work to marker, sl marker, k to end of rnd.
Cont in this manner until rnd 19 is complete.

Shape thumb gusset
Next rnd Work rnd 20 of chart, k to last 3 sts, pm for gusset, M1, k1, M1, pm for gusset, k2—50 sts.
Work 3 rnds even.
Next (inc) rnd Work to gusset marker, M1, sl marker, k to 2nd gusset marker, M1, sl marker, k to end of rnd—2 sts inc'd.
Rep inc rnd every 4th rnd 4 times more—60 sts in rnd, 13 sts between gusset markers.
AT THE SAME TIME, when rnd 39 of chart is complete, rep rnd 39 for back of hand to fingers.
Next rnd Work to first gusset marker, remove marker, place 13 gusset sts on scrap yarn for thumb, remove 2nd marker, work to end of rnd—47 sts.
Next rnd K to thumb opening, pm, cast on 5 sts, k to end of rnd—52 sts.
Knit 1 rnd.
Next (dec) rnd K to thumb marker, sl marker, ssk, k2tog, k to end of rnd—50 sts.
Knit 1 rnd.
Next (dec) rnd K to marker, remove marker, SK2P, k to end of rnd—48 sts.
Work 2 rnds even.

Little finger

Next rnd K to 6 sts before palm marker, with 2nd ball of yarn, k12, cast on 3 sts, pm for beg of rnd.

Divide the 15 sts on 3 dpns and work in St st until little finger measures 2"/5cm.

Next (dec) rnd [K2tog, k3] 3 times around—12 sts.

Next (dec) rnd [K2tog, k2] 3 times around—9 sts.

Next (dec) rnd [K2tog, k1] 3 times around—6 sts.

Break yarn, leaving a long tail. Thread tail through open sts to close top of little finger.

Ring finger

With first ball of yarn, pick up and k 3 sts in cast-on sts for little finger, k31, with 2nd ball of yarn, work ring finger as foll: k5 from back of hand, k 3 picked-up sts, k5 from palm, cast on 3 sts.

Divide the 16 sts on 3 dpns, work in St st until ring finger measures 2¼"/5.5cm.

Next (dec) rnd [K2tog, k3] 3 times around, k1—13 sts.

Next (dec) rnd [K2tog, k2] 3 times around, k1—10 sts.

Next (dec) rnd [K2tog, k1] 3 times around, k1—7 sts.

Complete as for little finger.

Middle finger

With first ball of yarn, pick up and k 3 sts along cast-on sts for ring finger, k 6 palm sts, place next 14 sts on scrap yarn for index finger, cast on 3 sts, k 6 back-of-hand sts. Divide the 18 sts on 3 dpns and work in St st until finger measures 2¼"/5.5cm.

Next (dec) rnd [K2tog, k4] 3 times around—15 sts.

Cont to dec and complete as for little finger.

Index finger

With 2nd ball of yarn, pick up and k 5 sts along cast-on sts for middle finger, k rem 14 sts. Divide the 17 sts on 3 dpns and work in St st until finger measures 2¼"/5.5cm.

Next (dec) rnd [K2tog, k3] 3 times around, k2—14 sts.

Next (dec) rnd [K2tog, k2] 3 times around, k2—11 sts.

Next (dec) rnd [K2tog, k1] 3 times around, k2—8 sts.

Complete as for little finger.

Thumb

With original ball of yarn, pick up and k 3 sts along thumb opening, place 13 sts from scrap yarn on dpn. Divide the 18 sts on dpns and work in St st until thumb measures 1¾"/4.5cm.

Next (dec) rnd [K2tog, k4] 3 times around—15 sts.

Complete as for little finger.

Right Glove

With larger needles, cast on 48 sts. Join, being careful not to twist sts, and pm for beg of rnd.

Work in k1, p1 rib for 9 rnds.

Begin chart

Rnd 1 K23, pm for palm, work chart pat over 25 sts.

Work as for left glove to shape thumb gusset.

Shape thumb gusset

Next rnd K2, pm for gusset, M1, k1, M1, pm for gusset, work rnd 20 of chart—50 sts.

Complete as for left glove. ❖

LACE PATTERN

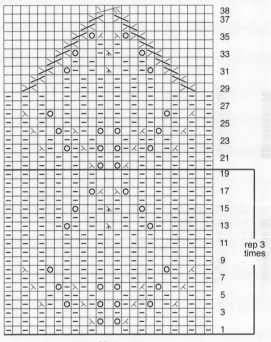

25 sts

Stitch Key

☐	k on RS, p on WS	⅄	SK2P
⊟	p on RS, k on WS	⧄	2-st RC
⊠	k2tog	⧅	2-st LC
⧄	ssk	⧅⧄	3-st RC
⊙	yo		

Vertebrae Stitch Afghan

Vertebrae Stitch Afghan

Lacy leaves emerge from spines against a stockinette background in a cozy blanket knit in two colorways.

Designed by Margeau Soboti

Skill Level:

■■■□

Materials

- Seven 1¾oz/50g balls (each approx 109yd/100m) of Noro *Silk Garden* (silk/mohair/wool) each in #267 (A) and #269 (B) **5**
- Size 9 (5.5mm) circular needle, 32"/80cm long, OR SIZE TO OBTAIN GAUGE

Knitted Measurements

Width 46"/117cm
Length 60"/152.5cm

Gauge

16 sts and 16 rows to 4"/10cm after blocking over chart pat using size 9 (5.5mm) needles. TAKE TIME TO CHECK GAUGE.

Stitch Glossary

ssk and p Ssk, return resulting st to LH needle, pass 2nd st on LH needle over 1st st and sl st back to LH needle—2 sts dec'd.

Stripe Pattern

*[2 rows A, 2 rows B] 4 times, 16 rows B, [2 rows A, 2 rows B] 4 times, 16 rows A; rep from * for stripe pat.

Note

Afghan is worked back and forth in rows. Circular needle is used to accommodate large number of sts. Do not join.

Afghan

With A, cast on 186 sts.
Next row (WS) Knit.

Begin chart and stripe pat
Next row (RS) Working in stripe pat, [k1, p1] twice, k4 [work 25-st rep of row 1, k4] 6 times, [p1, k1] twice.
Next row (WS) [P1, k1] twice, [p4, work 25-st rep of row 2] 6 times, p4.
Cont in this manner until row 8 of chart is complete. Rep rows 1–8 until stripe pat has been worked 3 times total.
Cont in chart pat as established, work [2 rows A, 2 rows B] 4 times, 16 rows B, [2 rows A, 2 rows B] 4 times.
Next row (RS) With A, purl.
Bind off loosely purlwise. ✤

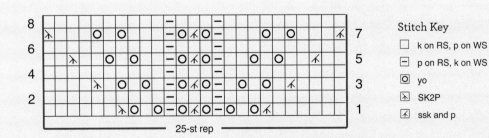

Stitch Key

☐ k on RS, p on WS
⊟ p on RS, k on WS
⊙ yo
⋏ SK2P
⋀ ssk and p

25-st rep

Textured Mittens

(page 34)

Wavy Stolette

(page 42)

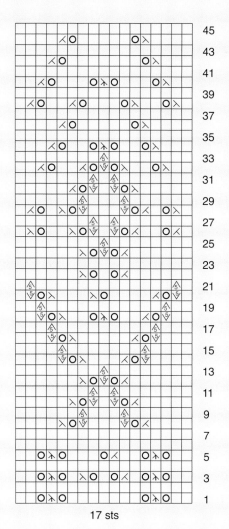

45
43
41
39
37
35
33
31
29
27
25
23
21
19
17
15
13
11
9
7
5
3
1

17 sts

Stitch Key

□	knit
⊠	k2tog
⊠	ssk
Ⓞ	yo
⋏	SK2P
ꟿ	MB
⋀	k5tog

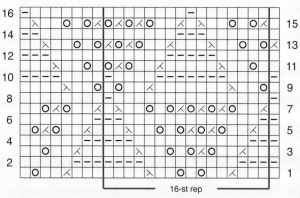

16
14
12
10
8
6
4
2

15
13
11
9
7
5
3
1

16-st rep

Stitch Key

□	k on RS, p on WS	⊠	ssk
−	p on RS, k on WS	Ⓞ	yo
⊠	k2tog		

Drape Front Blouse

(page 46)

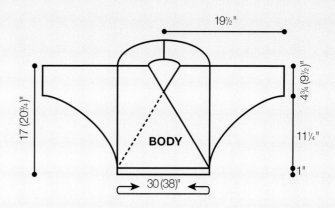

Faux Cable Mitts

(page 64)

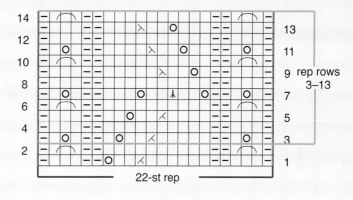

Stitch Key

☐	k on RS, p on WS	Ⓞ	yo
⊟	p on RS, k on WS	⋏	S2KP
⟍	k2tog	⌒	sl 1, k2, psso
⟋	ssk		

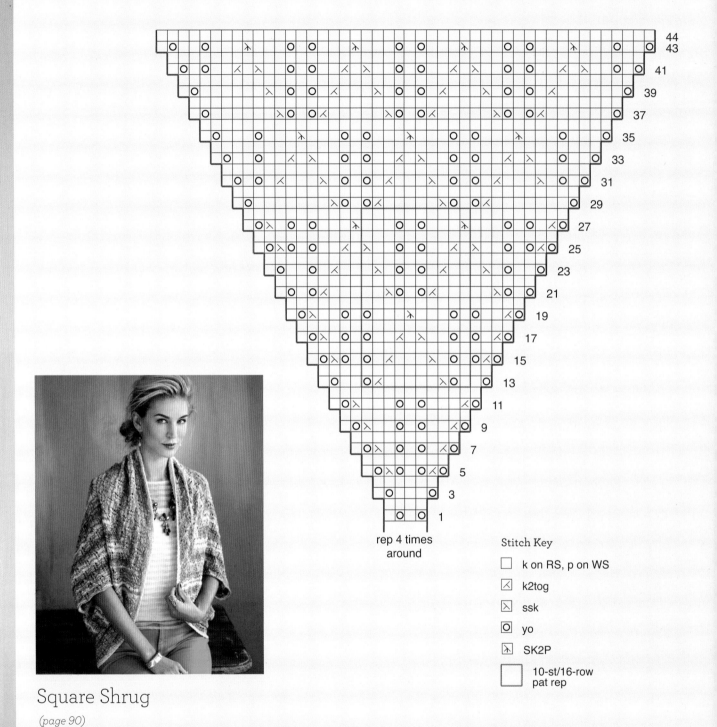

rep 4 times
around

Stitch Key

☐	k on RS, p on WS
◺	k2tog
◹	ssk
⊙	yo
⋏	SK2P
☐	10-st/16-row pat rep

Square Shrug

(page 90)

Circular Shawl

(page 114)

Leather-Trimmed Tote

(page 118)

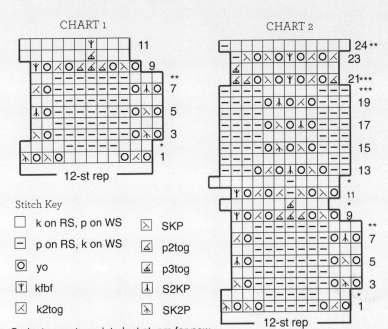

CHART 1

11
9
** 7
5
3
* 1

12-st rep

CHART 2

24 **
23
21 ***
*** 19
17
15
13
* 11
* 9
** 7
5
3
* 1

12-st rep

Stitch Key

☐	k on RS, p on WS	⟋	SKP
▬	p on RS, k on WS	⟍	p2tog
◯	yo	⟋	p3tog
Ⓨ	kfbf	⟰	S2KP
⟍	k2tog	⟍	SK2P

* On last repeat, work to last st, pm for new beginning of rnd, removing previous marker.

** At end of rnd, remove beg-of-rnd marker, k1, pm for new beg of rnd.

*** At end of rnd, remove beg-of-rnd marker, p1, pm for new beg of rnd.

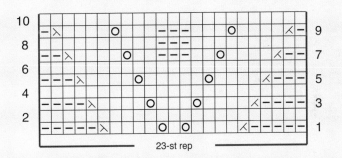

10
8
6
4
2

9
7
5
3
1

23-st rep

Stitch Key

☐	k on RS, p on WS
▬	p on RS, k on WS
⟍	k2tog
⟋	SKP
◯	yo

Floral Pointed Scarf

(page 122)

CHART 1

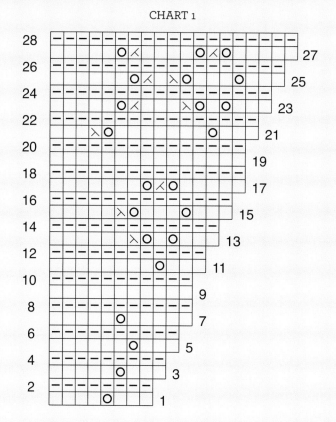

CHART 2

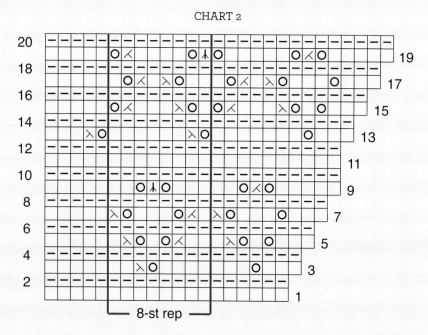

— 8-st rep —

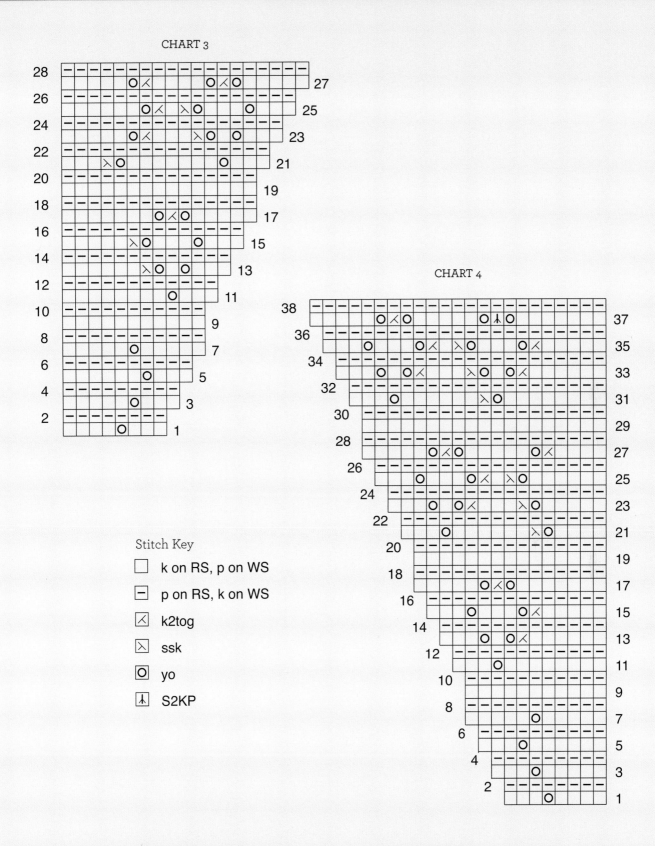

CHART 3

CHART 4

Stitch Key

☐ k on RS, p on WS

─ p on RS, k on WS

╱ k2tog

╲ ssk

O yo

⅄ S2KP

Helpful Information

Abbreviations

approx	approximately
beg	begin(ning)
CC	contrasting color
ch	chain
cm	centimeter(s)
cn	cable needle
cont	continu(e)(ing)
dec	decreas(e)(ing)
dpn(s)	double-pointed needle(s)
foll	follow(s)(ing)
g	gram(s)
inc	increas(e)(ing)
k	knit
k2tog	knit 2 stitches together
kfb	knit into front and back of stitch
LH	left-hand
lp(s)	loop(s)
m	meter(s)
MB	make bobble
MC	main color
mm	millimeter(s)
M1 or M1L	make one or make one left (see glossary)
M1 p-st	make 1 purl stitch (see glossary)
M1R	make one right (see glossary)
oz	ounce(s)
p	purl
p2tog	purl 2 stitches together
pat(s)	pattern(s)
pm	place marker
psso	pass slip stitch(es) over
rem	remain(s)(ing)
rep	repeat(s)(ing)(ed)
RH	right-hand
rnd(s)	round(s)
RS	right side(s)
S2KP	slip 2 stitches together knitwise, knit 1, pass 2 slip stitches over knit 1 for a centered double decrease
SK2P	slip 1 knitwise, knit 2 together, pass slip stitch over the knit 2 together for a left-slanting double decrease
SKP	slip 1 knitwise, knit 1, pass slip stitch over
sl	slip
sl st	slip stitch
ssk	slip, slip, knit (see glossary)
ssp	slip the next 2 sts one at a time purlwise to RH needle, insert tip of LH needle into fronts of these sts and purl them together
sssk	see glossary
st(s)	stitch(es)
St st	stockinette stitch
tbl	through back loop(s)
tog	together
w&t	wrap and turn
WS	wrong side(s)
wyib	with yarn in back
wyif	with yarn in front
yd	yard(s)
yo	yarn over needle
*	repeat directions following * as many times as indicated
[ ]	repeat directions inside brackets as many times as indicated

Checking Your Gauge

Make a test swatch at least 4"/10cm square. If the number of stitches and rows does not correspond to the gauge given, you must change the needle size. An easy rule to follow is: To get fewer stitches to the inch/cm, use a larger needle; to get more stitches to the inch/cm, use a smaller needle. Continue to try different needle sizes until you get the same number of stitches in the gauge.

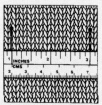

Stitches measured over 2"/5cm

Rows measured over 2"/5cm

Skill Levels

■□□□
Beginner
Ideal first project.

■■□□
Easy
Basic stitches, minimal shaping, and simple finishing.

■■■□
Intermediate
For knitters with some experience. More intricate stitches, shaping, and finishing.

■■■■
Experienced
For knitters able to work patterns with complicated shaping and finishing.

Knitting Needle Sizes

U.S.	Metric	U.S.	Metric
0	2mm	10	6mm
1	2.25mm	10½	6.5mm
2	2.75mm	11	8mm
3	3.25mm	13	9mm
4	3.5mm	15	10mm
5	3.75mm	17	12.75mm
6	4mm	19	15mm
7	4.5mm	35	19mm
8	5mm		
9	5.5mm		

Standard Yarn Weight System

Categories of yarn, gauge ranges, and recommended needle and hook sizes

Yarn Weight Symbol & Category Names	**0** Lace	**1** Super Fine	**2** Fine	**3** Light	**4** Medium	**5** Bulky	**6** Super Bulky
Type of Yarns in Category	Fingering 10 count crochet thread	Sock, Fingering, Baby	Sport, Baby	DK, Light Worsted	Worsted, Afghan, Aran	Chunky, Craft, Rug	Bulky, Roving
Knit Gauge Range* in Stockinette Stitch to 4 inches	33–40** sts	27–32 sts	23–26 sts	21–24 sts	16–20 sts	12–15 sts	6–11 sts
Recommended Needle in Metric Size Range	1.5–2.25 mm	2.25–3.25 mm	3.25–3.75 mm	3.75–4.5 mm	4.5–5.5 mm	5.5–8 mm	8 mm and larger
Recommended Needle U.S. Size Range	000 to 1	1 to 3	3 to 5	5 to 7	7 to 9	9 to 11	11 and larger
Crochet Gauge* Ranges in Single Crochet to 4 inch	32-42 double crochets**	21–32 sts	16–20 sts	12–17 sts	11–14 sts	8–11 sts	5–9 sts
Recommended Hook in Metric Size Range	Steel*** 1.6–1.4mm Regular hook 2.25 mm	2.25–3.5 mm	3.5–4.5 mm	4.5–5.5 mm	5.5–6.5 mm	6.5–9 mm	9 mm and larger
Recommended Hook U.S. Size Range	Steel*** 6, 7, 8 Regular hook B–1	B–1 to E–4	E–4 to 7	7 to I–9	I–9 to K–10½	K–10½ to M–13	M–13 and larger

*GUIDELINES ONLY: The above reflect the most commonly used gauges and needle or hook sizes for specific yarn categories.

**Lace weight yarns are usually knitted or crocheted on larger needles and hooks to create lacy, openwork patterns. Accordingly, a gauge range is difficult to determine. Always follow the gauge stated in your pattern.

*** Steel crochet hooks are sized differently from regular hooks: the higher the number, the smaller the hook, which is the reverse of regular hook sizing. This Standards & Guidelines booklet and downloadable symbol artwork are available at YarnStandards.com.

Glossary

as foll Work the instructions that follow.

bind off Used to finish an edge or segment. Lift the first stitch over the second, the second over the third, etc. (U.K.: cast off)

bind off in ribbing Work in ribbing as you bind off. (Knit the knit stitches, purl the purl stitches.) (U.K.: cast off in ribbing)

3-needle bind-off With the right side of the two pieces facing and the needles parallel, insert a third needle into the first stitch on each needle and knit them together. Knit the next two stitches the same way. Slip the first stitch on the third needle over the second stitch and off the needle. Repeat for three-needle bind-off.

cast on Placing a foundation row of stitches upon the needle in order to begin knitting.

decrease Reduce the stitches in a row (that is, knit 2 together).

hold to front (back) of work Usually refers to stitches placed on a cable needle that are held to the front (or back) of the work as it faces you.

increase Add stitches in a row (that is, knit in front and back of stitch).

knitwise Insert the needle into the stitch as if you were going to knit it.

make one or make one left Insert left-hand needle from front to back under the strand between last stitch worked and next stitch on left-hand needle. Knit into back loop. One knit stitch has been added.

make one p-st With the needle tip, lift the strand between the last stitch worked and the next stitch on the left-hand needle and purl it. One purl stitch has been added.

make one right Insert left-hand needle from back to front under the strand between last stitch worked and next stitch on left-hand needle. Knit into front loop. One knit stitch has been added.

no stitch On some charts, "no stitch" is indicated with shaded spaces where stitches have been decreased or not yet made. In such cases, work the stitches of the chart, skipping over the "no stitch" spaces.

place markers Place or attach a loop of contrast yarn or purchased stitch marker as indicated.

pick up and knit (purl) Knit (or purl) into the loops along an edge.

purlwise Insert the needle into the stitch as if you were going to purl it.

selvedge stitch Edge stitch that helps make seaming easier.

slip, slip, knit Slip next two stitches knitwise, one at a time, to right-hand needle. Insert tip of left-hand needle into fronts of these stitches, from left to right. Knit them together. One stitch has been decreased.

slip, slip, slip, knit Slip next three stitches knitwise, one at a time, to right-hand needle. Insert tip of left-hand needle into fronts of these stitches, from left to right. Knit them together. Two stitches have been decreased.

slip stitch An unworked stitch made by passing a stitch from the left-hand to the right-hand needle as if to purl.

stockinette stitch Knit every right-side row and purl every wrong-side row.

work even Continue in pattern without increasing or decreasing. (U.K.: work straight)

work to end Work the established pattern to the end of the row.

yarn over Making a new stitch by wrapping the yarn over the right-hand needle. (U.K.: yfwd, yon, yrn)

Distributors

To locate retailers of Noro yarns, please contact one of the following distributors:

UK & EUROPE
Designer Yarns Ltd.
Units 8–10
Newbridge Industrial Estate
Pitt Street
Keighley BD21 4PQ
UNITED KINGDOM
Tel: +44 (0)1535 664222
Fax: +44 (0)1535 664333
Email: **alex@designeryarns.uk.com**
www.designeryarns.uk.com

USA
Knitting Fever Inc.
315 Bayview Avenue
Amityville, New York 11701
Tel: 001 516 546 3600
Fax: 001 516 546 6871
www.knittingfever.com

CANADA
Diamond Yarn Ltd.
155 Martin Ross Avenue
Unit 3
Toronto, Ontario M3J 2L9
Tel: 001 416 736 6111
Fax: 001 416 736 6112
www.diamondyarn.com

DENMARK
Fancy Knit
Hovedvjen 71
8586 Oerum Djurs Ramten
Tel: +45 59 4621 89
Email: **roenneburg@mail.dk**

GERMANY / AUSTRIA /
SWITZERLAND/
BELGIUM / NETHERLANDS/
LUXEMBOURG
Designer Yarns (Deutschland) GMBH
Welserstrasse 10g
D-51149 Koln
GERMANY
Tel: +49 (0) 2203 1021910
Fax: +49 (0) 2203 1023551
Email: **info@designeryarns.de**

SWEDEN
Hamilton Yarns
Storgatan 14
64730 Mariefred
Tel/Fax: +46 (0) 1591 2006
www.hamiltondesign.biz

FINLAND
Eiran Tukku
Makelankatu 54B
00510 Helsinki
Tel: +358 503460575
Email: **maria.hellbom@eirantukku.fi**

NORWAY
Viking of Norway
Bygdaveien 63
4333 Oltedal
Tel: +47 51611660
Fax: +47 51616235
Email: **post@viking-garn.no**
www.viking-garn.no

FRANCE
Plassard Diffusion
La Filature
71800 Varennes-sous-Dun
Tel: +33 (0) 385282828
Fax: +33 (0) 385282829
Email: **info@laines-plassard.com**

AUSTRALIA/NEW ZEALAND
Prestige Yarns Pty Ltd.
P.O. Box 39
Bulli, New South Wales 2516
AUSTRALIA
Tel: +61 24 285 6669
Email: **info@prestigeyarns.com**
www.prestigeyarns.com

SPAIN
Oyambre Needlework
SL Balmes, 200 At. 4
08006 Barcelona
Tel: +34 (0) 93 487 26 72
Fax: +34 (0) 93 218 6694
Email: **info@oyambreonline.com**

JAPAN
Eisaku Noro & Co Ltd.
55 Shimoda Ohibino Azaichou
Ichinomiya, Aichi 491 0105
Tel: +81 586 51 3113
Fax: +81 586 51 2625
Email: **noro@io.ocn.ne.jp**
www.eisakunoro.com

RUSSIA
Fashion Needlework
Evgenia Rodina, Ul. Nalichnaya, 27
St. Petersburg 199226
Tel: +7 (812) 928-17-39,
(812) 350-56-76, (911) 988-60-03
Email: **knitting.info@gmail.com**
www.fashion-rukodelie.ru

Index